Black
Religion,
Black
Theology

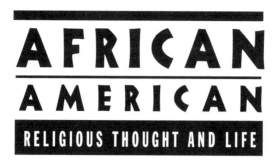

AFRICAN AMERICAN
RELIGIOUS THOUGHT AND LIFE

This series provides opportunity for African American scholars from a wide variety of fields in religion to develop their
insights into religious discourse on issues that affect African
American intellectual, social, cultural, and community life. The
series focuses on topics, figures, problems, and cultural expres-
sions in the study of African American religion that are often
neglected by publishing programs centered on African American theology. The AARTL program of publications will bridge
theological reflection on African American religious experience
and the critical, methodological interests of African American
religious studies.

SERIES EDITORS
ANTHONY B. PINN, Macalester College, St. Paul, Minnesota
VICTOR ANDERSON, Vanderbilt University, Nashville,
Tennessee

Making the Gospel Plain
edited by Anthony B. Pinn

A Private Woman in Public Spaces
Barbara A. Holmes

Dark Salutations
Riggins R. Earl, Jr.

Black Religion, Black Theology
edited by David Emmanuel Goatley

Black
Religion,
Black
Theology

THE COLLECTED ESSAYS
OF J. DEOTIS ROBERTS

Edited by
David Emmanuel Goatley

TRINITY PRESS INTERNATIONAL
A Continuum imprint
HARRISBURG • LONDON • NEW YORK

Trinity Press International, P.O. Box 1321, Harrisburg, PA 17105

Trinity Press International is a member of the Continuum International Publishing Group.

Unless otherwise indicated, Scripture quotations are taken from the Revised Standard Version of the Bible, copyright 1946, 1952, 1971 by the Division of Christian Education of the National Council of the Churches of Christ in the USA. Used by permission.

Scripture quotations marked NEB are taken from *The New English Bible.* Copyright © 1961, 1970, 1989 by The Delegates of Oxford University Press and The Syndics of the Cambridge University Press. Reprinted by permission.

Cover art: Photograph courtesy of J. Deotis Roberts

Cover design: Trude Brummer

Library of Congress Cataloging-in-Publication Data

Roberts, J. Deotis (James Deotis), 1927–
    Black religion, Black theology : the collected essays of J. Deotis Roberts / David Emmanuel Goatley, editor.
        p.   cm. – (African American religious thought and life)
    Includes bibliographical references (p.   ) and index.
    ISBN 1-56338-398-5
    1. Black theology. 2. African Americans – Religion. I. Goatley, David Emmanuel. II. Title. III. Series.
    BT82.7.R578 2003
    230′.089′96073 – dc21

                                                              2002156722

Printed in the United States of America

03   04   05   06   07   08   10   9   8   7   6   5   4   3   2   1

To generations of students
who have probed my mind and exchanged ideas.
It is hoped that those who have studied with me
will carry on the quest for religious knowledge
to inform their lives and those to whom they minister.

—J. Deotis Roberts

Contents

Part Five
THEOLOGICAL REFLECTIONS

Acknowledgments

We wish to express our appreciation to those persons who made this publication possible. The project was initiated in a conversation with Professor Anthony B. Pinn, co-editor of the African American Religious Thought and Life series by Trinity Press International. Professor Victor Anderson readily supported the project as well.

The editorial director of Trinity Press International, Henry Carrigan, has in many ways encouraged the publishing process. Amy Wagner, managing editor, has been incessant in her expert editorial preparation of the manuscript. All these persons deserve a vote of thanks.

Introduction

Theology done right is characterized in part by humility. I advance this assertion for two primary reasons. The first is related to the subject of theology, and the second is related to the one who does theology.

The subject of Christian theology is God. Any human endeavor to understand God and the things that have to do with God (i.e., God's identity, God's activity, human responses to God, and the like) should invoke caution and tentativeness. After all, to do theology is to tread on holy ground, and to tread on holy ground is inherently to risk trampling on the holy with unholiness.

Theology done right is not the self-assured pronouncement of opinions cloaked in a claim of the prophetic. There is something idolatrous about wholesale claims of accurate interpretation of the things of God that hide behind notions of inerrancy and infallibility. Even when one holds to the claims of the inerrant and infallible Word of God, those qualities do not transfer to the human interpreters and proclaimers.

Neither is theology arrogant assessments concerning the ills of society and the offering of alleged objective, yet simplistic, solutions in the face of complicated conditions. Problems are complicated by definition. Consequently, it seems rather peculiar for one to respond rapidly, and sometimes recklessly, to complex issues with easy answers. I do not there are no elemental responses to the complexities of life and thought. But saying that something is elemental is not the same as saying that something is easy. Further, claiming to have an elemental response to the multidimensional challenges of contemporary life ought to be done cautiously. This is so because of the second issue related to the necessity of theology characterized by humility.

Those who do theology are human. That fact alone is enough to demand a certain provisionality in things spoken about God. Even those of us who have a high regard for and a commitment to the concept of revelation must constantly be mindful that while God may show a thing, humans are the ones who view, respond to, and speak of that thing. Further, the very nature of our humanity carries with it a kind of inarticulateness. There is an inherent stumbling and stuttering in human existence that must always be acknowledged. While humans are said in the Psalter to be created a little less than God (or gods), we are definitively "less than." Thus, even our perfect praise is less than perfect, and our firmest grasps are less than sure. Whereas the treasure we hold is a priceless treasure, we hold the treasure in "earthen vessels." Consequently, overconfident theologians tend to make one nervous, sometimes nauseous. Primarily, if one has reverence for the holiness of the subject of theology, how can he or she speak with such confidence of the One about whom we can only begin to move toward understanding? The incomprehensibility of God ought to bring about humility in that which is spoken of concerning God. Secondarily, if one is honest about those who do theology, one surely is called to the warning "Proceed with caution." Hence, theology done right is characterized in part by humility.

Theology done right is also dynamic. Theology is not fixed. If it were fixed, it would be stagnant. Theology cannot be fixed because of the integrated involvement of the subject of theology and the ones who do theology. Theology is not theology without God. Neither is theology theology without humans. Therefore, even those committed to the idea of the immutability of God must concede to the hypermutability of humanity. Even if God does not change, God's stability cannot compensate for human instability. This is as true as the fact that God's sanity cannot compensate for the often horrific and demonic character of human insanity in sin. There is a mutuality in theology, an interrelatedness, a reciprocity of activity. Thus, theology must, because of the human participation in the task, be dynamic.

Because of the mutuality of divinity and humanity in the theological task, there are only two ways for a theology to be fixed, and both are related to death. First, theology may be fixed because that theology is dead. Second, a theology may be fixed because of a misunderstanding of the work of a dead theologian unable to explain to a subsequent generation what he or she was trying to say or do. When neither of these two conditions exists, theology, by definition, is dynamic, fluid, moving, growing.

Movement in theology translates into a continuum of discovery, rediscovery, and refinement. A living theologian (which all Christians are to some degree) encountering the living God, then, is discovering things about the theologian and the relationship with God. As God reveals Godself through Scripture and experience, the theologian stumbles upon treasures old and new. And even when a theologian has been engaged intentionally in the task for many years, there is the exhilarating experience of rediscovering truths and insights that come through the "many dangers, toils, and snares." Further, the discoveries and rediscoveries of a seasoned theologian open the way to reconceptualizing and refining the theological insights and implications that have evolved through the years. Consequently, a living theology is an emerging theology, and a living theologian is an emerging theologian open to the newness of the Spirit and the continuing creativity of the Creator God. These characteristics of humility and dynamism typify the work and life of J. Deotis Roberts.

This book is a compilation of writings by J. Deotis Roberts. The collection consists of selected essays and articles that have appeared in theological journals over a period of three decades. Included are writings that address diverse issues with insightful analysis, interdisciplinary research, and perceptive

applications. Readers of this volume have at their disposal
an invaluable resource that offers a sampling of the theological pilgrimage of Roberts, provides a historical theological
reference for the development of black theology, and fur-
nishes a theological reference in conversation with numerous
disciplines inside and outside of Christian theology.

This volume is produced partly as a tribute to J. Deotis
Roberts. In July 2003 Roberts turned seventy-six years old,
and the publication of this collection is one gesture to express
gratitude for his invaluable contribution to the academy, the
church, and the world.

Roberts is a first-generation African American theologian
who has been a pioneer of black theology as a distinct discipline. Of course, black Christians were doing theology long
before the introduction of black theology, but not until the
late 1960s was black theology introduced to the world in a
category of theological studies. Since the introduction of black
theology, Roberts has consistently been one of its most profound proponents. Unfortunately, however, he has not been
celebrated as the stellar theological figure he truly is.

Roberts's undervaluation by many is related to at least
three issues — his choice of institutions in which to serve,
the priority of his theological orientation, and his personal
disposition. Roberts has spent the majority of his academic
career in predominantly and historically African American
institutions of higher education. None of these institutions
grants a doctor of philosophy degree in theology. This has
had a twofold result. Positively, Roberts has demonstrated his
commitment to African Americans by teaching and adminis-
trating in black institutions, placing him squarely in the light
of African American culture and allowing him to be influential
in the preparation of untold numbers of ministry leaders in
African American Christian congregations and communities.
This consistent vocational choice, however, has meant that
Roberts has not had direct supervisory responsibility for numbers of African American Ph.D. students. This role would have

positioned him to influence their theological formulations in more advanced and telling ways. Having Ph.D. students under his direct supervision would have resulted in a greater dissemination of his methodology by professors of theology and religion. Hence, no second-generation college, university, or seminary professors bear the indelibility of Roberts's thought in their theological development.

Second, Roberts's entire career has been oriented as a theologian in service to the church. This does not imply that he has had little interest or influence in the academy. His deep involvement in academic guilds, his administrative duties as both dean and seminary president, his numerous publications, his international lectures, and the like clearly point to his commitment to academic excellence as well as the exchange of ideas with intellectuals. But those who know Roberts understand that his primary commitment is service to the church. It is not that Roberts has had a constricted idea of scholarship; rather, his scholarship has not been intended exclusively for the academy. He has desired his scholarship to influence the nature of the church, the academy, and the world toward the end of participating in the kingdom of God.

Third, Roberts has been more interested in service than personal promotion and self-aggrandizement. Those who take the path of service for the sake of service and refuse to promote themselves often are destined to be considered less seriously than they should be. Roberts is the proverbial gentleman and a scholar. Those who are impressed by shock value and superfluous rhetoric miss the import of those who speak with a sometimes subtle substance and astute analysis. This does not suggest that Roberts is easily dismissed. What it does suggest, however, is that one must be interested in depth and breadth to comprehend and appreciate the kind of theology done by Roberts.

This volume does not claim to be definitive or exhaustive. To provide such would require more pages than are contained herein. What this volume does is provide a glimpse of the evolving and expanding theology of one of America's best theologians. Tracing some of the movements of this theologian's work also can serve as a guide for the study of black theology. The book is organized by an understanding of Roberts's expanding approach as reflected in journal articles published during his long career. Consequently, students of black theology can use this work as a guide to the currents of general time periods. Such perusal will allow one to see more clearly analyses and proposals relevant to the theological, political, and cultural currents within this theological perspective and beyond. This explains the logic of the organization of the book.

The arrangement of works takes place in five movements. These movements reflect general trends in the thought of Roberts in a rough chronology. Of course, some overlapping is inevitable, but in general, the areas of concentration reflect an evolution in relationship to the developments of the issues and the theologian. The first division is "Theology and Politics: A Preface to Black Theology." Prior to the inauguration of black power in the late 1960s, Roberts's writings included reflections on the state and the necessity of the active engagement of individuals in politics to facilitate the creation of a more humane world. His ruminations include an analysis of the problem of discrimination and the measures that are called for in order to be a creative and redemptive society.

The second section is "Black Theology." Here is seen the beginnings of carving out a landscape on which to build a constructive theology. Efforts are made to call for interdisciplinary scholarship and a voice of relevance to the disparate constituencies of African American communities. The way of black theology is to be applied theology, ethical theology, and contextual theology. Black theology is not subsumed within other emerging theological currents but maintains its own place among theological developments and demands a place among the recognized religions of the world.

The third segment is "Theology and the Church." Here Roberts articulates the genesis of a black ecclesiology. The mission of the church cannot be separated from the theology of the church. The exasperation of some who contend that the church is not relevant has to do with a lack of understanding of the engaged nature of the church that facilitates the realization of liberation for oppressed peoples.

Fourth is the category of writings titled "Theology and African Consciousness." Here Roberts explores African worldviews to inform his readers of African religions, theologies, and cultures. The serious appreciation for and application of Africanisms help him to articulate Christian theology by leaning into the past for help in facing the challenges and attaining the desires of the future.

The fifth area of writings is "Theological Reflections." The essays in this section are born from a mature Christian theologian who addresses crises in the world at large and in the preparation of people for Christian ministry.

As all theologians who dare publicly to present their theological proposals, J. Deotis Roberts has taken his share of criticism. The coexistence of liberation and reconciliation is integral to Roberts's theology. At this point some have chosen to critique him. Must one be committed to the simultaneous goals of liberation and reconciliation? Of course, theology ought to be liberating regardless of the perspective from which the theological task is approached. Theology should free and facilitate us to move continually toward a fuller realization of whom God is calling us to be and what God is calling us to do. Further, Christian theology ought to be reconciling because Christians are reconciled to God through Christ and are called to a ministry of reconciliation. However, some theological perspectives have felt, for an assortment of reasons, that Roberts has failed to grasp adequately the impossibility of reconciliation until liberation is fully, or at least more fully, achieved. Nonetheless, Roberts has heard, considered, and responded to these critiques with a firm commitment to

the liberation-reconciliation motif. His commitment to this
style of theology may be related to his style of hermeneutic
that seeks a middle passage mediating between hypertheorists
and extreme pragmatists.

While Roberts may be criticized for his elemental commitment to liberation and reconciliation, he cannot be chided
for the lack of theoretical underpinnings for his theological program. Some trends in contemporary theology seem to
intend a departure from attention to theory. While developing
theory for the sake of developing theory is not a particularly useful exercise in the theological task (especially from
the perspective of those who must resist the efforts of mar-
ginalization), theologians cannot easily shake off the call to
establish a firm theoretical underpinning for the theological
task. Otherwise, they become vulnerable to being blown in
any direction. Theologians risk being convinced by whichever
position may be most persuasively articulated or contributes
neatly to their own sense of comfort and confidence. Thus,
theory is imperative and attended to in Roberts's work.

Roberts seeks to find a hermeneutical position that is appropriately balanced, though not statically fixed, between metaphysical philosophy and pragmatic theory. Roberts avoids
pure metaphysicism because of its tendency to avoid relating
adequately to the functional realities of human existence. This
metaphysical approach lends heavily from reason and turns
away from experience. Thus, in the search for the universal
principles of life and truth, metaphysicism can leave one dubi-
ous and insolent toward contextualization. To the contrary, a
rigid pragmatism is likewise averted; one's context ought not
to be the ultimate authority for all definition and critique of
one's existence. Pragmatism is suspicious about the validity
of transcontextual critique. What Roberts seeks to do herme-
neutically is to move toward theological comprehension and
articulation in a manner that takes seriously one's existential
context yet remains open to dialogue with partners in other
contexts. This approach reaches for the best of both worlds

in a theological program. This hermeneutic approach does not devalue the contextual influences on perspective, and it avoids imposing one worldview in a hegemonic fashion. Hence, what is desired here is a theory that is practical. Saying there is a practical nature to Roberts's hermeneutic is saying that he is aware that reason does not supersede emotion, that the universal and particular are inextricably woven, and that theory and practice belong together in such a manner that if one is considered decidedly superior, irreparable harm is done to the entire hermeneutical method, which in turn ruins the theology task.

The writings in this volume represent the broader corpus of Roberts's writings that relate the practical and theoretical, Christianity and world religions, theology and philosophy, particularity and universality, church and academy, contextualization and transcontextualization. That he intentionally interacts within what some would call polarities gives a particular strength to his contributions. This is a logical and natural approach for Roberts because of the holism of his way of being. This holism is manifest in his serious engagement with both the African and European aspects of African American heritage. Roberts is thoroughly African American. He seeks to lean into each aspect of his heritage to cultivate a blend of the benefits of both traditions. Hence, he is well versed in both European and African heritage. He values cultural context and western tradition. He holds that one must confront and process the realities inherited from both traditions. He does this, however, without being compromised. The resulting theology born out of this kind of being is deep and broad, profound and prophetic. It is related to the tension born of the "twoness" reflected in the writings of W. E. B. Du Bois. It produces a challenging and stimulating theology that calls one to action on behalf of the oppressed to seek liberation and reconciliation. It is a truly African American theology come of age.

My efforts in editing this volume have been taken on with fascination as well as a degree of frustration. The fascination

is related to the reading and rereading, arranging and rear-
ranging, including and excluding numerous essays and articles
from more than thirty years. The frustration is related to having to leave the majority of Roberts's writings out of this
collection.

While all of the articles contained herein are the works of
J. Deotis Roberts, the fact that I have selected and organized
the flow of this compilation means that I have assumed the
task, to some degree, of interpreting Roberts. I have chosen to
leave the writings in the language of each article's development
that adds, I believe, to the dynamic of Roberts's evolution
and emergence. Therefore, issues such as inclusive language
should be considered in the context of the day of its writing.
Roberts's maturation has brought about his emergence as a
strong advocate of inclusion of women in all aspects of scholarship, academia, and the church. Further, the arrangement
of topics reflects a continuing emerging from details of political engagement to discourse with world religions to universal
experiences of suffering.

In some ways this has been for me an overwhelming task
because this volume may serve to define J. Deotis Roberts for
many readers. I urge you, however, not to accept this work
as the defining piece with which to interpret Roberts. To the
contrary, may this volume serve as an introductory text to the
theological program of a gifted theologian that can stimulate
interest in further investigations into both black theology and
the theologian James Deotis Roberts.

Part One

Theology and Politics: A Preface to Black Theology

Chapter 1

A Theological Conception of the State

Our age has been noted for its political upheavals. If faith is relevant to the problems that confront man in this troubled sphere, it must speak redemptively. The burden of this essay is to present a theological conception of the state, that is to say, to point out the relevance of theology to political thought and action.

The State in the Christian Tradition

As one looks at the Christian faith in historical perspective, he notes that the Old Testament prophets had a concern for social issues. To them God was the Lord of history. It followed that God was the Father of all men and that the proper relation between men was one of justice and mercy. Though Amos and Isaiah concerned themselves with politics in a timeless message, they imparted no clear directives for present political problems.

When one turns to the New Testament, one receives from Jesus a clear statement that we should "render therefore to Caesar the things that are Caesar's, and to God the things that are God's" (Matt 22:21). His message of love for God and man provides a framework within which to conceive a

Originally published in *Journal of Church and State* (4 May 1962): 66–75.

political order. Jesus leaves room for the structure of the political order to grow out of the contemporary needs. Paul asserts that political authority is given by God. To Peter government is designed to restrain the evildoer. John of the Apocalypse describes Rome as the Antichrist and conceives the state as demonic. Though the general emphasis in the New Testament is eschatological, there is to be found there sufficient "realized eschatology" for a summons to this age.

As we move into the postbiblical period of Christian history, we observe two opinions concerning the nature and function of the state. On the one hand, there is the disposition to accept fully the apostolic doctrine that the powers that be are ordained by God. On the other hand, there is the apocalyptic outlook, which regards the state as being under the influence of demonic deities. To Tertullian, as to most Christians of his time, Rome was only an expedient of the Almighty. Yet at the same time, Tertullian and others boasted of the steady infiltration and conquest of the Roman Empire by Christianity. They asserted that even before Constantine the principles of the Christian Roman Empire were embedded in its pagan predecessor.[1] The baptism of Constantine led to a marriage of convenience between church and state without casting much illumination upon a theological conception of the state. But in Augustine we find a vital interpretation of the state.

Augustine's view of man in society may be termed realism. On the one hand, Augustine had a genuine understanding of the love that was the social bond of the city of God, but on the other hand, he depicted clearly the pride that characterized the city of this world. Pride was expressed socially and politically as the will to power and glory. The anarchy created by man's evil is so disastrous in its results that any force powerful enough to coerce these groups into some sort of order must be gratefully accepted. The state is thus a defense against sin. Its role is necessary but negative.

In general, there is a difference between Catholic and Reformation political thought. Catholicism emphasizes the Aristotelian idea of the state as an expression of the social nature of man and sees it as governed by the natural law that can be known through human reason. The Catholic distinction between the natural and the supernatural is the background for a doctrine of man that exempts man's nature, including his reason, from the worst consequences of the fall. Since the state belongs to nature, it shares this exemption. Man is in need of grace for his salvation, but this need does not imply as dark a view of his natural condition as we find in Augustine or the Reformers.[2]

Luther broke completely with the Catholic contrast between nature and supernature and with the view of nature as little damaged by the fall of man. But he had a dualism of his own that contrasted the preserving work of God through coercive political power with the saving work of God through the persuasive work of the gospel. Luther's position is a vindication of the independence of the gospel and the church. The church has its own way of working outside the sphere of political order. Luther insisted, nevertheless, that God is the Lord of the state and that rulers are responsible to him.

There is validity in Luther's realism about the conflict between Christian love and the necessary functions of the state, between what a man's duty may be in his office and what he would choose to do as a Christian in his private relations with his neighbor, but he separates these two realms so completely that there is no way of keeping the political order under the ultimate criticism of love. Luther's distinction between the Christian and the world and his suggestion that Christians do not need government are curious in view of his emphasis in other contexts on the sins of the redeemed.[3]

Calvin was clearer in the presentation of his view. He was closer to the Catholic view than Luther, in spite of his doctrine of total depravity. Underlying his explicit statements about magistrates and political institutions, there is a conception of the "common grace" that enables men to live together in civil society. Calvin has a remarkable confidence in man's capacity for political order. Given this view of man's capacity, it is not strange that Calvin held a positive view of the origin and function of the state. He concluded that the authority invested in kings and governors stemmed from the providence of God.[4]

Up to the Reformation there was a contrast in Christian thinking between those Christians who regarded the state as linked with the fall of man, as the divine provision for dealing with the consequences of sin, and those who, while not denying this negative role of the state, emphasized its positive functions as an instrument of human cooperation.

Contemporary thinkers are much harder to classify than the great traditions they represent. This was made clear in the Oxford Conference on Church, Community, and State in 1937. At the time there seemed to be a theological division in terms of geography between Protestants on the European continent and the whole Anglo-Saxon world. This was deceptive because there were wide differences among thinkers on the continent, but it was true that Anglo-Saxon theologians were on the side of the positive interpretation of the state's origin and function. They generally held a more hopeful view of human nature and took for granted the idea of a limited state.

The Anglo-Saxon view was generally represented by the following statement: "The moral obligations which are written in the conscience of all men are to be realized in the state. The state serves the divine purpose by realizing the ideals of humanity, freedom, equality, and universal well-being."[5]

Emil Brunner and Karl Barth are representative of the theological view concerning the state on the European continent. They differ considerably on the nature and function of the state.

Brunner, though a Calvinist in background, emphasizes the negative view of the state. He follows the distinction between the "orders of creation" and the "orders of preservation," and he classifies the state among the latter because the state is based upon the fall.[6] Brunner recognizes the necessity of the state as the consequence of original sin. The very fact that the state is necessary is a call to repentance. He is concerned less with the idea that the state comes into existence as a result of sin and more with the conviction that the state that exists to restrain sin becomes in an extreme way the embodiment of sin.[7] It would appear that Brunner's thinking about the state is controlled by his limited definition of the state as the agency of compulsion and also a tendency to draw an absolute distinction between even just forms of compulsion and the work of love.[8]

Barth's christological doctrine of the state leads in a different direction from Brunner's view. Barth's view is based on a refusal to separate the world as known through the doctrines of creation and sin from the redemptive work of Christ that has already taken place. Barth makes much of the idea that God used the state in the crucifixion of Christ, and that Pilate, without knowing it, played a part in the divine work of redemption. So the very event that is the demonstration of the state's cruel and unjust use of power is also the sign that it is not outside the sphere of redemption.[9]

Barth does emphasize the work of the state in dealing with sin, but the whole spirit of his discussion is different from that of Protestants who see only this side of the state and from Catholics who sharply separate the state, which belongs to the natural order, from the church, which belongs to the supernatural order. He makes clear his belief that the state should not seek to become the church, that it will never be the kingdom of God. The state bears a relative and provisional character. At times Barth appears to conceive of the state as making possible the freedom to preach and respond to the gospel.

Barth's view of the state includes a type of christocentrism that is problematic and perhaps confusing. And yet he helps

overcome some unwholesome tendencies in Protestant theology on the subject. For example, he gives some relief from
the hardened Lutheran dualism between the two realms that
leaves the state outside the sphere where there could be
a distinctively Christian criticism of politics. He overcomes
conservative conceptions based on the "orders of creation."
Barth's method is strained and often absurd since he attempts
to derive all the necessary political guidance from revelation.
He refuses to use principles of justice that have a broader basis
than the Christian faith.[10]

Reinhold Niebuhr has been clear on the need of the state
to overcome disorder and at the same time has shown how
the state can become an embodiment of pride in relation to
other states and a tyrant in relation to its own citizens. He
has pointed out the fact that a relatively good state, in pursuit
of peace and justice, is limited by its sinfulness in its exercise
of power. It is limited also by the moral deficiencies of the
people of the nation as a whole in their approach to the needs
and aspirations and fears of other nations. He is a constructive
critic of the American way of life so often equated by Americans with Christianity itself. He unearths the irony of both
communism and democracy, for both Russia and America in
their self-righteous garbs may be described as innocent nations
in an innocent world. But to the extent that they think more
highly of themselves than they ought to think, in the light of
the ethic of love they require criticism and judgment by the
Christian faith.[11]

The attempt has been made to look at the theology of
politics through the insights of a group of representative theologians in Christian history. I have been somewhat arbitrary
in my selection, but I believe that through a cursory examination of these theologians I have captured the spirit of
Christian opinion on this subject. It remains for me to work
out a concise formulation of my own theological conception
of the state.

Toward a Theological Conception of the State

The state is a primal factor in the structure of human society. The state is implicit in the earliest forms of human life. The state provides for security against internal and external foes. It belongs to God's purpose in creation. Some critics of the state contend that it had no place in original humanity but was a later artificial product. The assumption underlying this theory is that what is "natural" in its origin has a higher degree of authority than any institution that owes its rise to deliberate human initiative. A fundamental question that has consequently arisen with reference to the state has had to do with its origin. Was it a natural growth or an artificial creation? If the purpose of the state is clearly conceived and deliberately carried out, it may be said to be "artificial." If, on the other hand, it comes into being as the result of dispositions operating more or less automatically, it may be said to be "natural."

In the light of this distinction, my conclusion is that the state is both natural and artificial. There must have been more or less conscious and deliberate purpose in its formation. But back of this purpose there were involuntary social and political needs that sought satisfaction. They have their rootage in our human nature. Man, as Aristotle put it, is a "political animal." There are in him state-forming dispositions that are deeper than volition. It may then be said that the state has its ultimate foundation in human nature rather than in the human will and hence may be regarded as a natural growth and from the religious point of view as an order of creation.

The psychological needs that enter into the foundation and structure of the state are numerous. But two in particular make the state a practical necessity. One of these is the need of fellowship or community. The need is innate and is rooted in God's creative purpose. Men are by disposition gregarious. Sociability is inherent in them. Men are born to live together, and apart from this sense of community they would not be truly human. The state is the broadest expression of full community life, apart from humanity itself, and in this respect is necessary to a complete satisfaction of human sociability.[12]

The state also meets the need for justice as it relates to human relations. Without justice there can be no security, peace, or cooperation. To establish justice is therefore of primary importance in human life, and to do so is the distinctive function of the state.[13]

According to Albert C. Knudson, power belongs to the very essence of the state.[14] Machiavelli was the first to formulate this doctrine distinctly. He subordinated morality wholly to the state's quest for power. Power with him was ultimate. It needed no moral justification. Heinrich von Treitschke accepted Machiavelli's dictum that the state is power and became the brilliant and influential exponent of it in Germany, but he regarded the state as having a moral function and being in itself an ethical force and a high moral good. To uphold the fatherland was with him an unconditional moral duty. Obedience to the state took precedence over the dictates of the individual conscience.[15]

Brunner's position may be recalled at this point. He asserts that the fundamental character of the state is not right but might, and it belongs to the very essence of the state that it should have the power to compel obedience. Compulsion, however, is in itself contrary to love; it is sinful, "demonic." Yet without this demonic power of compulsion, the state could not come into existence or fulfill its divinely appointed purpose in and for society. The state is a necessary evil. It is a product of collective sin, a consequence of original sin, which we as Christians must accept as both an act of discipline and an act of repentance.

There is a danger that this theory may be used as a justification of unwarranted aggression or as a basis for social and political pessimism. The implication is to the effect that every state is in its essence a nonmoral exerciser of power.

Over against this pessimistic concept of the state, which subordinates justice to power, is a more optimistic and ethical view. According to this view, the state had one of its chief roots in the need for justice, a need that could be met only by the possession of sovereign power. But the power came second, not first. It was not power that created right but rather right that created power. In other words, the power of the state is instrumental. The state has its source in the need for a just and secure social order, an order that can be realized only through the exercises of sovereign power. The unethical use of power is not inherent in the nature of the state. Good and evil are mixed in the state as in the individual. The ethics of the state differ in some respects from those of the individual, but there is no reason to ascribe demonic possession to the state. It is misleading to speak of "moral man" and "immoral society" in purely contrasting terms.[16] The state is the collective will, and as such there is no reason why it, as well as the individual, should not be capable of being moralized. Apart from individuals the state is an abstraction. It follows that the individual alone is concrete and that the moral principles of the state reflect those held by the individuals in the state unless the state is totalitarian and there is no voice from the *demos*. Even then the moral principles in the state will be those of the individuals in power. Thus, the state is a moral agent.[17]

The use or direction of power determines its moral content. It may be used for evil or good ends. Sovereignty, then, does not mean absolute and unlimited power. It involves the rule of reason and conscience. It implies a recognition of the normal interests and rights of men and the duty of the state to protect these rights and interests. Instead of seeking to suppress or absorb them, the true state will rather encourage their development insofar as they minister to the physical and spiritual welfare of the people. Its own supreme authority will cooperate with the lesser authorities embodied in every normal and progressive human society. The state is to provide a context within which men shall have room to lead the good life.[18]

Conclusion

As noted above, the early fathers of the church either accepted the apocalyptic attitude toward the state of the Apocalypse of John or the more positive attitude of St. Paul. The latter view was more influential. On the one hand, the state is conceived of as a result of man's sin. Its fundamental function is negative — it is designed to restrain the evildoer. On the other hand, the state is conceived of as an instrument for good here and now — though its role will terminate at the end of the age and it is never to be identified with the kingdom of God. The former position is close to Brunner's; the latter is akin to Barth's. Brunner's view is based on the distinction he makes between love and justice. His view is reminiscent of Luther's conception of the state. Barth is christocentric in his treatment of the subject but shares the Augustinian position as transmitted through the system of Calvin.

It appears that a combination of the two traditional views of the state may be desirable. Man is a sinner in need of redemption. But at the same time, God has created man for fellowship. In order to realize a life in community consistent with God's creative purpose, the institutionalization of human relationships is necessary. Thus, the state is ordained by God for this age, both to restrain the evildoer and to make a good life in the community possible. It has the power to exercise authority as the supreme authority over the temporal affairs for this age, although it has no right to ask of its citizens the loyalty that belongs to God or to suppress the wholesome function of smaller groups that contribute to the general well-being of the citizens of the state. However, when these interest groups are in conflict, and as a result the welfare of the larger group is endangered, the state has the right and the authority to administer justice and bring about reconciliation between individual groups in order that the good life may be available for all. The role of the state is to "hinder the hindrances" to the good life.

The conclusion is that the state in its collective composition and through its citizens should conceive of its origin, purpose, and destiny as being of God. It is an order of creation in that it is ordered by God to fulfill both creative and redemptive objectives. The God who finds a place for this organization of human life in community desires for all men the abundant life. This implies that Christians who are not only children of creation but adopted sons of God by the saving work of Christ are to relate their faith to political issues and assume a responsible citizenship to the end that in this present age — "the times between the times" — our eschatological hopes may become to the greatest extent possible a realized eschatology. Though the kingdom of God in its fullness may not be a realizable possibility, and to that extent a "possible impossibility," our goal must at this present time — in the here and now — be "a laboring together with God" to the end that the kingdom of this world may become "the kingdom of our God and his Christ."

Chapter 2

Christian Conscience
and Legal Discrimination

This essay is concerned with the role the Christian conscience should play in overcoming legal discrimination. I am among those who feel that the greatest threat to a segregated way of life is an aroused Christian conscience that condemns it. It is unfortunate that religion has not been more influential in this regard. My hope is that set forth here will be some suggestion as to how Christians may make their witness against segregation more effective.

The Christian Conscience

If we start with the view that human nature can be changed or remade and that it is neither inherently good nor evil, we may assume that conscience is subject to growth and direction. Thus, prejudice based on the myth of racial superiority is not inherited but acquired. The deeply rooted character of racial prejudice may be explained by the fact that it is transmitted by example and precept to children during the most impressionable years of their development. Furthermore, it is a form of collective sin. Reinhold Niebuhr is right, I believe, when he points out that conversion is more efficacious in setting us free from individual sins that defy common standards of decency than collective sins that are imbedded in the folkways and

Originally published in *Journal of Religious Thought* 19, no. 2 (1962–63): 157–61.

mores of a static culture.[1] Often religious beliefs are brought into play to support prejudices, and good Christian men stand in church pulpits to preach their doctrines of racial superiority with no feeling of hypocrisy. Race attitudes "formed under the aegis of caste are therefore defended with a peculiar tenacity and with complete self-righteousness."[2]

The Christian conscience is divided. A church official in a ministerial meeting in Little Rock during the racial crisis there put his finger on the problem thus: "There are Christian people who feel that segregation is right and there are Christian people who feel that integration is right."[3] In the same crisis one pastor called on his flock to remove prejudices from their minds and legal hindrances from the statute books that stand in the way of full citizenship for Negro citizens.[4] Another pastor said, "Just as sure as I know my own name, separate facilities for whites and Negroes — these are things pleasing to the Lord."[5] At the same time the Ministerial Alliance called a prayer meeting for peace, another group of ministers wanted to be certain that peace did not include integration. In order to be sure, they called another prayer meeting in the interest of segregation and the support of Governor Faubus. Thus, we have conscience against conscience, prayer against prayer. In such a deadlock in the sincere convictions of the devout, who is to judge?

This seems to me to be where those who do not subscribe to an infallible conscience have an advantage. To begin with, the assumption that our consciences do not come ready-made from God but that he provides us with a potential moral nature that will be shaped by our own decisions and our social environment seems to be the best way out of the dead-end street of conflicting consciences among Christians who are equally devout. The conscience must be nurtured and "schooled" in Christian principles. In this sense conscience must be conceived of as a "relative instrument" and therefore subject to continual growth. Herein one may discern the role of law as a "schoolmaster" both to impart knowledge and to expose guilt. Law in this sense becomes a kind of means of grace in that it serves to create outwardly the conditions within which the Christian community can be built.[6]

Legal Discrimination

Segregation by law has not led to mutual benefits for both races. It became a power instrument of white domination. "Separate but equal" means "separate and unequal": in public facilities, education, transportation, and economic opportunity. Here is an example of "the perversity of human pride in taking practical exceptions to its own professed standard of value in order to serve its own interests."[7]

The Supreme Court's ruling against racial segregation in public schools continues a trend that began more than a hundred years ago. Although history reveals advances and setbacks for the Negro, the legal trend has slowly moved toward Constitutional changes, legislative actions, and judicial decisions favoring equality for all American citizens.[8] This has been the prevailing emphasis of the highest legal tribunal in the United States, but its status and decisions have not gone uncontested.

The supporters of state rights contend that the Supreme Court has been both arbitrary and totalitarian in its school desegregation decision. On the part of some, there may be a genuine misconception of the nature and the meaning of the Constitution. There may be a question as to the scheme of power, both legislative and judicial, that the Constitution set up between the nation and the states. According to Crosskey, the role of the Supreme Court is to defend the national rights of citizens under the Constitution, and the role of the government of the states is to be subsumed under the Constitution.[9]

While such technical problems as the nature and meaning of the Constitution and the jurisdiction and authority of the

Supreme Court may cause some difficulty, the real problem of implementing decisions dealing with equal rights for Negroes stems from a different source. It is the deliberate attempt to circumvent these civil rights decisions for political or prejudicial reasons. Those who are in the grip of racial bias may be sincere in their defense of legal segregation out of moral blindness, for prejudice and discrimination are closely related.[10] On the other hand, interposition as it has been applied by local courts in relation to the school desegregation decisions appears to be mainly a political tool. It serves as a ready-made basis for perpetuating office holders who hold the favored view or for placing others in office. It is designed to persuade, not lawyers, but the electorate at large by appealing to deep-set emotions. Interposition is a kind of emotional catharsis for millions of segregationists who feel that an accustomed way of life with all of its status and security is being arbitrarily snatched away from them. They see no appropriate substitute for the "unwritten constitution of custom" that has been violated. This leads to resentment against the Supreme Court.

Beach has made a searching criticism of the purpose of interposition. It is one of those frantic attempts to circumvent the Supreme Court's action of 1954 in the school decisions, whether legal or illegal — moral or immoral. Negatively, interposition means that the states have a right to interpose their sovereignty to challenge what they consider to be unconstitutional acts of the federal government. It means essentially the same thing as nullification. It has to do with the obvious appeal of state rights of the Tenth Amendment. It does not point out the conflict between civil rights and state rights of the Fourteenth Amendment. Positively, it enables the states in their separate sovereignties to protect their public schools while avoiding integration. The Virginia Gray Plan and the North Carolina Pearsall Plan are examples of this attempt.[11]

Ever since the rendering of the *Plessy* decision, sincere Christians have tried to support the separate but equal position on moral grounds. A distinction was made between race distinction and race discrimination. That is to say, separate but equal schools would be an example of racial distinction but not of racial discrimination. It was asserted that race distinction connotes a difference and nothing more, while discrimination necessarily implies partiality and favoritism. Race distinction is race consciousness rather than a sense of superiority by the predominant group.[12] The Honorable Clyde R. Hoey in a speech before the 81st Congress asserted that the federal government has no right to interfere with state segregation policies since the Constitution of the United States does not say that segregation is discrimination.[13] Such theories are interesting but rather unconvincing to those who have been the victims of a system of legal segregation. To the oppressed group no distinction — legal or moral — may be discerned between race distinction and race discrimination or between segregation and discrimination.

Conclusion

The conscience of sincere Christians, having been informed by the fundamentals of the gospel, can do what the law cannot do. The Christian way in race relations may be viewed as a supplement to the work of just law. And when the law is just, it can create a climate of change in which proper laws may be enacted. Moderation is not a proper stance for an awakened Christian conscience. In this regard the "children of darkness are wiser than the children of light." Pro-segregationists are deeply devoted to their cause and have plans for the future. Those who are aware of the evils of segregation by virtue of their Christian convictions cannot avoid the issue. They cannot expect time to heal the wounds, nor may they be silent, for this will be against the cause of social justice. Men of goodwill must be busy with a plan to enact laws and create a true fellowship based on the Magna Carta of Christian liberty: "All are one in Christ."

Part 2

Black Theology

Chapter 3

Black Theology and the Theological Revolution

Martin Luther King Jr. has rightly observed that the church has often been a taillight rather than a headlight! We may observe further that even this taillight is lighted not autonomously by the church from the inside but by a crisis or trauma bringing pressure on the church from the outside. A case in point is the *Black Manifesto.* Most churches have not been willing to respond directly to the *Manifesto* but have been aroused to do more humanitarian work as a result of this document. Once again the church, as an institution, has been a taillight (seeking the easier way out rather than the more generous) and been aroused from without rather than from within.

If this is true of the church, it is equally true of theologians who interpret the faith of the Christian church. The social and moral conscience of theology has registered mainly the crisis situations or the traumas of the age that have shaken the church from without. There is a real question as to whether "frontline" theology has really been in the forefront. In this regard, the black church and black theology are not exceptions. Theology has usually been a response rather than an initiator of ideas and action. Thus, the crisis-response syndrome operating in our society characterizes most thought and action associated with the theological enterprise.

Originally published in *Journal of Religious Thought* 28, no. 1 (spring–summer 1971): 5–20.

Death-of-God theologies have been based on the optimism of "man come of age," who rejoices in his strengths and who no longer needs a deus ex machina or "god of the gaps." They are an essential response for the crisis resulting from a loss of transcendence amid affluence and technological breakthroughs. Black theology is likewise a response to black protest beginning with the 1960s but coming to full flower in 1966 with the cry for black power. Black theology is a theological response to a crisis precipitated by the black revolution of the decade now come to a close. The effective witness of the black church and the survival of Christianity among blacks is bound with a worthy theological reflection on the black religious experience.

Harvey Cox, who manages to stay alive in the theological revolution, surviving the disappearance of many giants and martyrs from the scene, moves chameleon-like from one theological fashion to another. Cox combines considerable knowledge of theology with knowledge of the behavioral sciences and humanities. He is uniquely equipped for rapid adaptability to new currents in the theological revolution. He is young and popular. Cox sees great potential in three movements that he considers "almost providentially prepared to solve the problem of theological poverty and religious ruination." According to Cox, these movements include radical theology, which emphasizes human creativity, experience, and the imaginative transcription of symbols; the theology of hope, which through its futuristic orientation has what Cox calls "political vision"; and finally, secularization theology, which grasps meaning in sociocultural realities and uncovers within them their implicit theological dimensions.[1]

Cox points to what he calls "personal style" and "political vision" as the two secular goals of contemporary theology. Concerning the first goal, personal style, Cox points to a new religious sensibility, the comic élan, the spirit of festivity and fantasy that one finds at the creative edges of churches and in the religious underground.[2] As perceptive as Cox is, he does not recognize black theology as one of the most creative currents in the entire theological revolution. This should not surprise me, for in a recent book on religion and nationalism in America, nothing was said about the religious motivation behind black nationalism in America. Though this work was sent as a complimentary copy, it was somewhat of an insult since I had reminded the general editor personally of the need to include the black experience in future publications. These examples point up to the need for theological explorations into black religious history and thought. Cox, by exploring the black religious experience, would have discovered that celebration and political vision have been present constantly in this tradition. These are not on the edge of black religion or driven underground. They are at the center of black faith and worship.

As a "secularist," Cox's fame has survived the death of the death-of-God theologies. Though he was associated with the death-of-God theologians, he was not identified with them. He is rather an interpreter of the broad-based secularism of our time. Most recently his wide interest has led him into another byway. If he followed the "social" instinct in his *Secular City,* he now appears more "psychological" in his *Feast of Fools.* More precisely, he is sociopsychological as he gives a theological interpretation of festivity or celebration by the analysis of what he calls the "comic élan." The concept of a "holy hippie" is somewhat amusing; it is rather surprising to see where some theologians are prepared to sprinkle "holy water." Perhaps this is another attempt to make contact with the now generation — especially the New Left. Theologically speaking, we all face a generation gap — more exactly, a credibility gap.

Black theology has a similar cleavage to overcome between Afro-American Christianity and the religion of black power. Little communication takes place between the "business as usual" black church and the militant black intellectual or his soul brother on the turf. If Michael Novak, William Stringfellow, and Harvey Cox can speak theologically to the New

Left, the underground church, and the secular-minded Jew —
to WASP and Roman Catholic "alumni" and "dropouts," the
black theologian has a mission to black militants who have
given up on the church. Furthermore, because his indigenous
theology is unwritten, he must speak to black Christians and
black churches as well. It is clear that if he does not speak, no
one else cares enough. Perhaps no one else can or will speak.
It follows that he must.

A word of caution is needed both for the black theologian and for theologians like Harvey Cox. They must seek to
be true to their conviction concerning the revelation given to
them. They must not distort the message. In these times the
mission to theologize comes as a witness to faith — even as a
prophecy. We must be aware that now, as of old, prophecy
can be *false* as well as *true*. Joseph R. Brandt is correct, I
believe, when he observes: "A search has been taking place
for some time to discover a meaningful way for the Church
to communicate with the world. Everything from jazz masses
to God-is-dead theologies has been tried. Repeatedly, these
new methods have either failed to speak in an understandable
language or have distorted the gospel beyond recognition."[3]

The age of systems theology is past. Multivolumed works
like those produced by Tillich, Brunner, and especially Barth
do not hold the field. A problem-oriented tendency in theology is emerging. Most constructive theologies are preoccupied
with some salient concern of the theologian or his age, and
in many instances, the man and his age. Some new theologies appear to be faddish — at least on the surface. A second
look, however, often leads one to realize that a deep question
is haunting the theologian and his generation. While this may
be obvious for existential theologians who wear their feelings
on their sleeves, it is not so apparent in reference to radical
and secular theologians inspired by Dietrich Bonhoeffer.

The death-of-God theologies are bred in deep yearning for
meaning and fulfillment in the secular city of affluence and
technology. It is a situation in which God is not so much *dead*

as man is *alive*. Secular city theology is characterized by the fact that man has come of age, cut the umbilical cord, and in all honesty has decided that God is not "up there." It is a theology of strength — it is for the suburbs, for the "haves" — it does not know powerlessness, injustice, and bondage!

Black theology is "inner-city" theology. Whereas the white church often suffers "suburban captivity," the black church suffers "slum captivity." Even if the black man enjoys a secular city socioeconomic status, he has numerous soul sisters and brothers in the dark ghetto. These are not merely members of his race; they are blood relatives. The cleavage between town and gown, academy and church, is being overcome as theology finds its way into colleges and universities as well as into living rooms and the streets. It is my concern that this popularization of theology be more than a fancy. Theology now has an opportunity to meet the deep needs and longings of men as they face the real problems of living. I see the mission of a black theology in this deeper sense as it reflects on "black awareness," "black pride," and "black power." Richard Wright, in his essay "The Man Who Lived Underground" (adapted from Dostoevsky's *Notes from the Underground*), has described in a profound manner the plight of the black poor. Wright relates the agony of a black fugitive falsely accused of murder and brutalized by white policemen who ironically are sworn to enforce the law. The theological mission of the black theologian is to interpret the Christian faith in such a way that light may shine in his darkness and the darkness cannot put it out.

The black man who has escaped to the suburbs is partially exiled from his own people. He usually belongs to the first generation to move into the mainstream. The best part of him may still remain with his loved ones. In a real sense, he cannot escape until their escape is possible also. His elevation is paralleled by the demotion and degradation of millions of his brothers who are bound in "slum captivity." A strange thing is happening. Black parents long to forget their past, but their children refuse to allow them to forget. Vincent Harding refers to Stanley Saunders, formerly of Watts.[4] Saunders, as a Rhodes scholar and Yale law student, confessed that he had attempted to hide from his white friends the truth of his origins in the ghetto of Watts in order to gain acceptance and assimilation into American society. But when he became aware of his blackness and proud of it, he makes an affirmation that is representative: "If there is no future for the Black ghetto, the future of all Negroes is diminished. What affects it, affects me, for I am a child of the ghetto. When they do it to Watts, they do it to me, too. I'll never escape from the ghetto. I have stacked my all on its future. Watts is my home."[5]

It is in some sense fortunate that black theology can join the contemporary theological movement. The reading public is used to rapid seasonal changes in theology. On the other hand, it will be unfortunate if what black theologians have to say is considered to be of temporary worth. It is worthy of note, however, that much recent theology has been "hyphenated" to life. It has been "applied" or "ethical" theology. In addition, much theology has been culture-oriented. Theology has ceased to be primarily abstract and metaphysical. In the language of Unamuno, theology in recent years has dealt with men of "flesh and bone." Adversity and grace, sin and forgiveness, despair and hope have been discussed in the context of man's *Lebenswelt*. In a word, theology has become "situational" in a better sense than the so-called "situational ethics." Perhaps "contextual" carries a more wholesome meaning. This contextual approach to theological discourse, because it is "live" and rooted in experience, may turn out to be the best thing that has happened to theology. It may explain the "return to religion" and specifically the interest in theology on the part of laymen and youth. Thomas W. Ogletree, in summing up what he calls "the shifting focus of theological reflection," has this to say:

> It is a mark of the vitality of the Christian community that many persons in many different ways have been bold

enough to tackle these issues [problems faced by contemporary Christian theology] head on.... The unique
challenge of our time is to explore more fully the meaning of the Christian message as it addresses men at the
point of their strength in the midst of their political and
social involvements.[6]

Ogletree is very perceptive concerning what is happening
in the theological revolution. Affirmation of human manhood,
the movement from anxiety to responsibility, the awareness
of human strength, and the like belong to the radical shifts
in theological focus. But while these insights survey the general theological terrain, crucial aspects of the black experience
are untouched. Even the insights that are insightful must be
indigenized if they are to be useful. For example, the white
suburban Christian may have lost his faith because he has too
much. Their offspring are seeking the simple life because they
"had too much too soon." Affirmation of human adulthood is
vis-à-vis God. The black Christian, as object of charity and
victim of unjust treatment at the hands of fellow humans,
affirms his manhood vis-à-vis white men who have denied
his dignity as a person. Radical secular theology is characterized by "loss of transcendence" in reference to God. Black
theology speaks about overcoming a childhood imposed by a
paternalistic society. Black women joining the women's liberation movement should bear in mind that black men have been
"boys" all these years and perhaps they should be allowed to
be men before being robbed of their manhood. The passion of
black men to be men in society must not be denied them by
their wives. Eldridge Cleaver says, "We shall have our manhood. We shall have it or the earth will be leveled by our
efforts to gain it."[7]

We are, as black Christians, seeking to overcome the damage done to black men during slavery. The black family
has often limped along without a father figure. This has
been especially damaging to boys who need this identity. A

"big brother" is no adequate substitute for a good father. Unemployment and welfare programs have systematically robbed the black father of his proper image in his home. At a time when we are trying to unite the black family, black church, and black community, black men need the full understanding and support of their women and children. It is my impression that the women's liberation movement is basically a white middle-class phenomenon and that even elite black women will join the movement at their own risk. And that they may, in seeking to "liberate" themselves, hurt the cause of black "liberation" that depends on black men being men for the first time in the history of this republic.

What Ogletree has to say about political and social involvement will be the very lifeline of black theological reflection. But what he has to say about men being addressed in their strength needs modification. Black power is merely a hope, a dream for the future; white power is a present-day reality. Black theology is addressed to the powerless, to the "other America" victimized by the undisciplined and unchecked power grip of white America. The need for black power arises because of the unwillingness of whites to share power — or to relinquish the power for self-determination to minority groups. The contextual approach to this matter requires a particular understanding of God and man. A Christian humanism rather than a "Christian atheism" would appear to be more to the point. Rather than dealing with the silence and absence of God with man's strength, we need to speak more of a God who is present in power and is able to bring strength out of weakness. We assume that God exists and that he is a benevolent providential God. This God brings comfort and, by the agency of the Spirit, provides strength. But in biblical language, he also works upon "stony" hearts of oppressors and gives them hearts of "flesh."

The so-called theology of ecology needs some examination. If by environmental theology we are to deal meaningfully with creation and God as the author of nature, we are dealing with lasting concerns. If we are discovering foul air and polluted water for the first time because human life might not last on the planet for so many thousands of years, we are not yet with it. What about those who have been trapped for years in a walled society, who have been hemmed in by social, economic, political, and other barriers? What of blacks who moved "north of slavery," who left a situation of intolerable poverty as sharecroppers only to inhabit ghettos? A people who have lived in poverty, disease, and lawlessness and have shared their dwellings with rats and roaches, whose lives have been controlled by slumlords, caseworkers, and politicians, have known "pollution" for a long time. They have not just discovered it. The white *and* absentee control of their destiny must be replaced by a recognition of their manhood and the freedom and responsibility associated with it. In a word, concern for the human factor of creation must concern black theology before there can be any excitement over long-range environmental cleansing. Pure air is not the primary concern for people who don't know where the next meal is coming from!

The population limitations suggested by ecological theology do zero in on the black community. Christian theology is concerned with improving the *quality* of human life. A responsible concern for the future of children requires some real concern for those things that will make life worth living. Black theology, as it speaks of the dignity of human nature, must advocate responsible parenthood not merely for the sake of children but for racial betterment as well. The black community will not be strengthened by presenting a bumper crop of illiterate, homeless, and therefore powerless people, without skill, unemployed, and increasingly unemployable due to cybernation and automation. Add to this the further disabilities stemming from racism!

I am aware that there is a sentiment abroad that any curb on the birthrate of blacks is a subtle form of genocide. If blacks can be eliminated by limited births, these persons believe, in time the white man will be completely relieved of the "black presence." There will be no need for concentration camps, colonization programs, and the like if blacks will just stop having large families. My reply to this is that through all constructive means — through the exercise of black power, we should seek to improve the lot of black people economically, politically, socially — in every way. Since human life is precious, black people should treasure it. Families should be limited in keeping with the earnest desire to improve the experience of our children. In a word, we should seek to improve the quality of life for our children. Responsible parenthood may require us to limit the quantity of our family size to realize this end. No special restriction should be acceptable to black people regarding the number of children, especially if it is suggested by whites who may have questionable motives. But at the same time, good judgment and the welfare of our children and our people demand that we must limit our families. The irrational and irresponsible reproduction of children who will be victimized by all kinds of social ills and who in turn will victimize their own people in the course of time must be curbed. It is consistent with the purpose of black theology, namely, to make human life more human, to speak in this manner both to blacks and whites concerning the population explosion vis-à-vis the black community.

Charles Long of the Divinity School of the University of Chicago has recently moved toward a theological stance. He has made some interesting observations regarding the death-of-God theologians. He has noted that their writings tend to be provincial and assume Western culture to be the standard of civilized life. The movement is a reaction to the loss of meaning in the West. According to Long, they are "carrying on the hermeneutics of conquest," and their understanding of man is based on the "pre-eminence of *their* historical period and culture as the absolute arbiter of all human values." What we need, according to Long, is "a reflection upon the real meaning of death and the real meaning of life in the light of an inclusive understanding of mankind."[8]

Long goes on to point out that the death-of-God theologians seem to assert that oppressed people of the world believe that it was the will of God that they suffered from their oppressors. In such a situation, the death of God should be hailed as a sign of freedom and renewal of mankind. By wedding the notion of God to progress, they have been led astray. Long says:

> One might come to know the meaning of God through … that mystery of man which is precisely his humaneness, a mystery of man which calls upon us to decipher Him rather than manipulate Him. The meaning of God can have an authentic sense if we make it a part of a genuine hermeneutic which enables us to see how the mystery of man and his world is revealed in all situations — not just those of the West, but those of the past and those of the present.[9]

I have quoted extensively from Long, a black scholar, for two reasons. First, he is the only United States–born scholar known to me who is a recognized authority on the history of religions. He is therefore interested in a theological expression that reaches all men. I share his universal concern because history of religions is an avocation of mine. Second, Long's observations regarding the death-of-God theologians are similar to my own. I say amen to his assertion that the death-of-God theologies are "rationalizations in decadence." This comes close to my assessment that there is often a shallow faddism in the so-called "new theologies." Robert McAfee Brown has rightly observed that radical theologians were saying what we need is "love" until the Germans said what we need is "hope." He adds that perhaps what we really need is "faith."[10]

I have arrived independently at the conclusion that the death-of-God theologies do not make contact with "black

religious experience," that they spike to "haves" and not to
"have-nots," and that the real concern of black Christians centers not around the existence of God but around his character.
The moral attributes of God, in reference to the real experiences of evil and suffering, are of primary interest to black
Christians. The essential question for black Christians is not
Does God exist? It is rather Does God care?

But again I must stress the importance of Long's concern for
a universal theological expression. A theological stance growing out of black power can readily become not only separatist
but nationalistic as well. I share his interest in the theological
expression to the human race. What black theology has to say
has special relevance to the third world since the aftermath of
colonialism is not unlike the aftermath of slavery. James Cone,
the theologian of black power, is in danger of being hemmed
in by the implications of black nationalism to such an extent
that his radicalism may be blunted by his provincialism.

Right after Karl Barth's retirement from the chair of theology at Basle, Robert Clyde Johnson sought to introduce
Barth's successor in an essay entitled "Who Is Heinrich
Ott?"[11] It would be helpful if someone who knows Cone well
would write "Who Is James Cone?" Again I am reminded that
a perceptive black scholar has said that after LeRoi Jones, no
black art is possible, for he has expressed all the hostility of
the black man.

Jim Cone is a child of Little Rock. As a teenager, he confronted white power in its most brutal form. He is young,
perhaps under thirty. He is the first black theologian, to my
knowledge, ever appointed to a chair of theology in an outstanding white seminary. His graduate work centered around
a theological reflection on the black experience. In a real sense,
he is the right age, at the right time, in the right place. It would
be impossible for another theologian to articulate the anger
and frustration of black people better than Jim Cone. But in a
real sense, his role is demolition. Someone has to build a viable
statement of the Christian faith. On one hand, he has not

expressed this anger as well as some nontheological spokesmen. On the other hand, even his closest admirers, young seminarians, are now requesting that he move beyond demolition to theological construction. It remains to be seen whether he can overcome the self-imposed restrictions that limit his program. As a friend and close associate, I wish him well. We all await the fruit of his labors. Furthermore, it is my impression that the main burden of his course load is directed to the black religious experience. This may be due to his own choosing. It may be due to the blind spot in much liberalism that limits appointments of black scholars to black subjects. At any rate, the exposure to perspectives and resources needed for theological construction and maturation will be found in the broad field of theology and not merely in reflection on the black religious experience.

Black theology must speak to the black man on the plane of personal existence. This is the reason, I believe, why existentialism has a native affinity to black religious experience. I am going to illustrate one instance in which an understanding of this relationship is emerging. The question of the color of the existential Christ is merely the mythological or symbolical structure of a valid Christology for the black Christian. The *essence* or *content* of that Christology is another matter. The black Christ is for the *bene esse* or well-being of the black Christian, helping him overcome the identity crisis of his Christian life and experience. His relation to Christ can be understood in terms of personal pronouns. The content of the revelation of God in Christ can now make contact with the black man in his situation, though despised, rejected, and oppressed.

No white person can know what it means to be black by painting his skin, by working with black children, by having an interracial courtship, by living for one week on a welfare budget. All of these may improve sensitivity, but they are not the real thing. In some sense, they are artificial and may fool the individual into believing that he really understands what is involved more than blacks themselves. The black man inherits his skin color involuntarily and maintains it permanently. This becomes his lifelong identity badge in a racist society that rejects him on sight.

He is automatically branded as inferior, and there is no hiding place for him in this color-conscious society. Whereas his white friends may wash their faces, break ties of romance and friendship, leave the ghetto, move to suburbia — all at will, the black man may be trapped geographically in the ghetto if he is poor or rejected sociologically if he is affluent. The most difficult task for the black man is to obtain psychological freedom. If he can accept his blackness, be proud of it, and find meaning for his life, he can know true inner freedom. This is where Jesus, as the black Messiah, comes in. The black Messiah enables the black man to stand up to life. Henceforth the black man may be alone, but never lonely.

The black Messiah loves the disinherited. In the biblical record, Jesus is portrayed as one born in a barn, rejected by the religious and political establishment, and considered an outcast and a dear friend of sinners, harlots, and tax collectors. The do-gooders, the law-and-order people despised him, but the radicals and common people of his time loved him and hung on his words. He died on a shameful cross, accursed between two thieves. And yet God raised him and made him both Lord and Christ. This is our New Testament faith.

It is not difficult to understand why a black Christ who comes to the black man in his blackness and identifies with his lot can bring succor and comfort to the black man. In leading the black man to a deeper self-understanding, in Bultmann's terms, a black Christ also brings meaning, redemption, and power to all who receive him. He brings deliverance to captives, sight to the blind, hope to the hopeless.

Could not the blackness of the black Messiah be a type of hiddenness and yet revealedness of God, as Barth would put it? If God in the incarnate Word comes as man and if the Prince comes (as Brunner says) in beggar's garments, is it not conceivable that he comes to the black man in his blackness? Is the concept of God as *incognito* in the Word made flesh off limits to the black experience? Isn't it possible that God addresses each man and each people where they are in his/their human situation in a manner that is redemptive? These are ideas bandied about by theologians. May not black theologians try them on for size? Our problem centers around what Christ can mean to Christians in black skins in a racist society.

I have only sketched one instance in which existential insights may be employed by a black theologian in pursuit of his task. In this connection, because I do not espouse a literal black Messiah, I do not need to find black Jews. Albert Cleage, who holds such a view, has done violence to biblical history without scholarly justification. Cone employs existentialism as a method but selects Camus, who considered theology as intellectual suicide as his model. Also, Cone and Cleage appear to require that whites accept the Christ of the oppressed. This could very well create an identity crisis for whites. I would like to hold on to a universal Christ who reveals himself existentially as I have explained. The symbolism of the black Messiah is especially helpful for black Christians, but it does not deny the possibility that others may confront him in a different cultural and ethnic dress that is more significant for them. In a word, the universal and reconciling Messiah is also the black Messiah. In the experience of black Christians, his love is personal — entering into their life and faith.

If religious existentialism is helpful in the black man's search for meaning, revolutionary theology is most valuable as a protest ideology. The theme of liberation is attractive. Lest we assume that we are automatically moving toward violence, we are to be reminded that bloodless coups have characterized some of the most successful revolutions of our time. In some cases in which revolutions have been violent, the people have witnessed one blood bath after another and injustice has only changed hands. The nonviolent revolution offers reconciliation beyond confrontation and liberation of the oppressed. This I envisage as a proper Christian goal.

There is a political and revolutionary aspect to Ernst Bloch's philosophy of hope, and this is especially true of Jürgen Moltmann's theology of hope. Moltmann's thought is greatly inspired by the Christian-Marxist dialogue and has been intensified by his interest in civil rights in the United States. He was visiting professor at Duke when Martin Luther King Jr. was assassinated. He had just presented a position paper on the theology of hope to an assembly of theologians from across the country on the night that Dr. King was killed. On the following day, I asked Moltmann what this theology of hope had to say to a hopeless people. He admitted that his theology had been inspired by social and political problems in Germany and that the race problem had to be examined in the context of the history and sociology of America. It was then that the seed of "black theology" began to germinate in my own mind. It was Moltmann's conception of theology as "political" rather than the particular content of it that aroused my interest.

Paul Lehmann, as chairman of this important conference on Moltmann's thought, is not easy to understand. But when he does break through with meaning, he is worth pondering. The constant theme of Lehmann has to do with making human life more human. On this theme, Lehmann can be most radical and extremely revolutionary in his message to the church and to the world. This idea has real appeal and tremendous possibilities for black theology. It will be echoed throughout all that I have to say.

Professor Richard Shaull of Princeton Theological Seminary appears to be the most popular and persistent advocate of a radical theology of revolution in this country. He got his inspiration as he carried on a ministry in Latin America. According to Shaull, the liberal has been able to criticize the utopianism of the radical. But the liberal has not succeeded in breaking out of the present order's logic and in providing principles of social organization that offer a new possibility beyond the present contradictions. The danger of the radical is presenting "present impossibilities as possibilities." But the danger of liberalism is restricting its possibilities so that we have no clear way ahead. The liberal, therefore, ends up with a false brand of utopianism. He expects the present system to provide solutions of which it is incapable.[12]

Reinhold Niebuhr, still the political prophet of America, speaks out of retirement. What he has to say is worth airing here. He reminds us in a recent essay that America still suffers from three "prides" — the pride of power, the pride of virtue, and the pride of riches.[13] We are thoroughly convinced of the virtue of democracy and capitalism. We have a "manifest destiny" to maintain them whether they can be humanized or not. With Lincoln we assume the superiority of our government and refer to it as "the last best hope of earth." History, according to Niebuhr, has played an ironic trick on our pride. We denounce European monarchs as tyrants. But while the monarchs of Europe gradually lost their power, our presidents have become too powerful. They have become what Niebuhr calls "elected monarchs." The result of this is that we are in Vietnam. This tragedy has resulted from the fact that we love democracy, the fact that our president is commander-in-chief of the armed forces, and the fact that we have the money to spend on this senseless and undeclared war. Vietnam, according to Niebuhr, illustrates how pride of power, virtue, and riches has led us from irony to tragedy.[14]

I am attracted to Niebuhr for the manner in which he combines realism and vision. Richard Shaull, the theological New Left critic of Niebuhr, agrees with him that lovers of power are needed to shake up the status quo. Corrupt and obsolete institutions are not changed by moral suasion alone but by counterpressures, economic, social, and political.[15] Niebuhr, who wrote the theological masterpiece *The Nature and Destiny of Man*, had a profound theological understanding of individual man as well as social man. His realism regarding human sin led him to advocate not only radical changes in personal lifestyle but structural changes in institutions as well. Niebuhr constantly reminded us that love must be supported by the "pushing and shoving of justice." This has led a careful student of Niebuhr's thoughts to say:

> The Christian visionary is...by definition a realist. He knows that he is set down in a society that is radically out of kilter. That gap — between what is and what ought to be — fires him to action toward the future, but it saves him from the debilitating despair of the idealist who is unprepared for the shock of reality. Christian vision, at its deepest level, *is* Christian realism.[16]

A source close to President Nixon has served notice to all minorities that the president is taking a big gamble that no minority can ruin his political future. He expects to stake his political life on the silent majority located mainly in the South and West of this country. These forgotten or middle Americans come from those whom Colin Morris describes as the "un-young," "uncolored," and "unpoor." According to Richard Wilson, Nixon is the first president in thirty-seven years wholly free of minority support. He is determined that no minority (racial, youth, labor), no protesters, and no haters shall prevail over the legitimate interests of the majority.[17] It is against such realism that black theology must forge ahead.

Harvey Cox takes up the issue of the "police preventative war against the Panthers." He rightly points out the need for all Americans to be concerned by this trend. He says that the question of who controls the police has now reached a point of crisis. Police now form an almost independent subculture less and less responsive to the citizens they are supposed to protect. The Panthers have increased police antipathy in demanding local community control of police. Police, according to Cox, must not be empowered to make political decisions and carry out punishment left to the jurisdiction of courts.[18] Cox gets to the heart of the problem: "Many Americans, including Black Americans, disagree with . . . the Panthers. . . . Yet when a Hampton can be murdered in bed, every American is a little less secure. If having colleagues who are under indictment . . . is sufficient cause to bring upon massive police attacks, then who is really safe?" Cox adds, "Of course, being White helps, at the moment."[19] I am sure Cox would agree that if you are white, young, and radical, skin color may not help either.

As we close, let us be reminded that black theology will be ethical in a profound sense. Thus, the theological models for which we have responded most approvingly have been those that have been avowedly ethical and those that may use massive structures of power for human betterment. I am especially impressed by *A Theology of Human Hope* by Rubem Alves, a Brazilian disciple of Shaull, as he advocates a messianic humanism as a proper theological stance for the oppressed everywhere. The difference between a humanistic messianism and a messianic humanism is crucial for black theology to consider. In one case, a humanistic messianism, like Marxism, is limited to human resources that are fallible, sinful, and inadequate for the humanizing of life. On the other hand, a messianic humanism has the advantage of inviting the agency of divine grace and power into the human struggle for justice, but because it is a "humanism," it allows for human effort as well. Black theology reminds us that in the effort to make all human life more human, that we as Christians are "laborers together with God."

Chapter 4

Christian Liberation Ethics: The Black Experience

In a casual conversation with Jürgen Moltmann, in his office at the Protestant Faculty at Tübingen, I was led to certain valuable insights: (1) that in discussing human rights, we must include social rights as well as individual rights; (2) that black theology must look at its own roots in the racial wing of the Reformation, that is, Anabaptists; and (3) that we will have to do our own reflection and not rely on the conclusions of Euro-American scholars.

The black experience of the Christian faith has been different. Our response to the Christian faith has related to our experience of unmerited suffering as a whole people at the hands of fellow human beings, many of whom have confessed faith in the Christian God. Our response has deepened our spirituality and sharpened our socioethical consciousness. Therefore, we are aware that blacks have a profound contribution to make to Christian social ethics.

My main vocation is that of a theologian, but thus far blacks in the field of ethics are reluctant writers. The task will not wait. Black theology is in essence theological ethics with a strong awareness of the Bible as a primary source. In fact, the reading of the Bible in the light of the black experience is the foundation for the entire enterprise.

Liberation ethics as well as liberation theology are rooted in an experience of oppression in which a group of people

Originally published in *Religion in Life* 48, no. 2 (summer 1979): 227–35.

suffer; their suffering may be based on class, sex, or race. A liberation ethic emerging out of the black experience must be an ardent and uncompromising foe of racism. It cannot ignore class or sex as forms of oppression, but it must keep a single-eyed vision on racist oppression. Moving from this center of perception, it can and should be sensitive to, concerned about, and active in the alleviation of other forms of oppression. But its primary agenda must always be racism. Even when there are coalitions with other groups, the black agenda must be a root and branch attack against racism.

Sources and Methodology

William C. Settles Jr. writes about the religious survivals of slave revolts:

> The historical experience of African peoples with religion has been incantatory. Religious ideas have been the instrument of ritual and ritual the rhythm of being. Religious ideas have lived: they have been purposeful rather than mechanical, imminent rather than transcendent. On the Old Continent as well as in the new world of enslavement, religion has been invoked, called upon by the faithful and embodied by them.[1]

Settles compares the impact of religion on the Haitian slave revolution on 14 August 1791, with Nat Turner's Rebellion in 1831 in Southampton, Virginia. The plantation settings were different, but both regimes exploited Africans; and within these locations some leaders, through their understanding of their plight wedded with religious consciousness, had developed their ideas of liberation and dared to act on these to find freedom for their black followers.[2] A group of black religious scholars have written in a forceful manner regarding this protest characteristic of black religion since 1966.

Among these are Vincent Harding, Gayraud Wilmore, and
Eric Lincoln.

Charles Long has written about the essence of the religious
experience of the Afro-American. He describes Africa as a
religious image, the involuntary presence of blacks, and the
experience and symbol of God. Long goes so far as to suggest
that a new interpretation of American religion would result
from the careful study of the black religious experience.[3]

Long is joined by Cecil Cone, who is mainly concerned
about the celebrative characteristic of the black religious heritage. Cecil Cone does give some attention to the doctrine of
God as an almighty sovereign power in the black experience
of the Christian faith. In his critique of the "black power"
element in the thought of James Cone, Joseph Washington,
and myself, he exchanges the prophetic for the priestly, a price
too high to pay, for black religious experience contains both
in abundance. Fortunately, the writings of Howard Thurman
stand as a corrective to this one-sided view. As a master of
spiritual disciplines, Thurman has a deep social awareness
in his thought and life. This, I believe, flows from a profound reading of the black religious heritage. As a part of the
quest for understanding the Christian faith, the Bible was soon
embraced by black slaves. The Africans brought with them a
highly developed and sophisticated awareness of creation as
divinely ordered. Robert Bennett says: "With his deep sense
of God as creator, the slave heard in the Bible...not a new
word but ideas with which he was more or less familiar. The
new faith was not etched on a *tabula rasa* nor was it merely
seized upon as a means of survival."[4] Bennett sees in Scripture
the message that God acts in the course of human events to
bring about divine purposes for humankind. Our reading of
the Scripture, according to Bennett, is to the effect that it is
God's intention that humans are to be free and live in a just
society. Black awareness in black history is an assent to God's
justice within creation and an affirmation of God's lordship
within history. America's problem, therefore, is not the black

presence but the white refusal to accept that presence. Black theology, according to Bennett, has the task of developing a contemporary expression of salvation history. White racism and black suppression are to be brought together. Bennett concludes:

> The same hermeneutical process which confronts us with the message from Scripture also suggests those categories by which we can deal creatively with the word being spoken by the black experience. It is assumed that God's final self-revelation given in Jesus Christ and under the old and new covenant has consequences for the whole course of human history, and that word and event continue as a potent influence in conveying that revolution. As we deal with blackness and black history as potent word and event, we come to see Scripture as relevant. . . . It leads us to discern and accept God as speaking [in] our situation.[5]

Whatever we do with method, we must somehow bring the experience of ethnic suffering by blacks and the Christian ethic together. We must also keep the liberation motif at the center of our focus. The individual approach to ethics is inadequate. We cannot neglect personal piety and ethics. But we must develop a community ethic. Here Paul Lehmann's vision will be useful. Our context must be the African/Afro-American religious connection wedded to the biblical faith. The social analysis of Marx and Weber must help to provide structures and categories for our thought. The serious work of Martin Luther King Jr. must be mined and brought up to date in the post-black power era when we confront a new form of racism that is subtler and more stubborn and widespread than any variety of racism we have faced thus far. "New occasions teach new duties," and the black exponents of a Christian social ethic must be perceptive readers of the "signs of the times."

The Theological Basis of Human Rights

Jürgen Moltmann may well set the stage for this part of our discussion. In an essay on the theological foundations of human rights, Moltmann says:

> Human rights are ultimately grounded not in human nature; nor are they conditioned by individual or collective human achievements in history. They reflect the covenant of God's faithfulness to his people and the glory of his love for the church and the world. No earthly authority can legitimately deny or suspend the right and 'dignity of being human. It is in the light of this covenant as fulfilled in the cross and resurrection of Jesus Christ and in the power of the Holy Spirit outpoured upon all flesh that Christians express solidarity with all those who bear a human countenance, and more particularly, a willingness to stand up for those whose fundamental rights and freedoms are robbed.[6]

Moltmann's discussion hinges on these important considerations: (1) the equal dignity and interdependence of men and women; (2) the equal validity and interdependence of personal rights and social rights; and (3) the equal dignity and interdependence of the present and future generations. His theological argument is based on his explication of the biblical and theological understanding of the *imago Dei*. His orientation is Reformed, and the argument is cast in the mold of an exclusive christocentrism. His structures and confession of faith are, in my judgment, too limited to guarantee human rights for humanity as a whole, the majority of whom stand outside this confession. We need a cosmopolitan and humanistic understanding of revelation and ethics, similar to that provided by the Stoics in classical Christian thought, to meet our needs today. Indeed, the legal, political, and moral context for natural law and human rights is precisely this in a historic sense. The structures for ethical discussion by all who stand within the Barthian tradition to which Moltmann and James Cone both belong are too limited to meet the demands for a theological and ethical exposition of human rights for our time. Any black ethicist should clearly see that his ethical outreach should be beamed at the mass of black folk at home and people in the third world with whom he is wed by cultural ties, racism, and poverty.

As we look at the history of ethics, we find two American ethicists whose perceptions are helpful — Walter Rauschenbusch and Reinhold Niebuhr. Rauschenbusch had a keen awareness of social evils and applied the gospel in this direction. Unfortunately, he was too optimistic about human nature and too enchanted with American democracy to deal realistically with either. Furthermore, he did not isolate racism as a serious problem to be addressed. Glenn R. Bucher, writing on the omission of racism on the agenda of the advocates of the social gospel, tries to explain rather than excuse them. He argues that most of them, if not all, did their work in the urban north.[7] The fact that they did not readily link poverty with racism indicates that they were white rather than black.

But Rauschenbusch's importance for the black ethicists may well consist of two factors: (1) his awareness of the collective nature of evil and his willingness to initiate social reforms with the desire to bring the kingdom of God to earth; and (2) his advocacy of cross-bearing for the cause of social justice. He writes: "Social regeneration involves not only growth but conflict. The way to the Kingdom of God always has been and always will be a *via dolorosa*. The cross is not accidental, but is a law of social progress."[8]

Reinhold Niebuhr, on the other hand, is too pessimistic concerning human nature. He leaves us with many ambiguities in our moral perception. In protesting against liberalism, he swings, I believe, too far in the other direction. He ends up with a "possible impossibility" and an unfortunate cleavage between the manifestation of love and the pushing and shoving of justice. But along with that pessimism concerning man, there is a realism that the black ethicist needs to take quite seriously. One of the most helpful aspects of his thought is the distinction he makes between individual and social ethics. While I would hesitate to contrast the two, I am grateful for his separating these problems for definition and analysis. He argues for a sharp distinction between the moral and social behavior of individuals and of social groups — national, racial, and economic. This distinction, according to Niebuhr, justifies and necessitates political policies that would be necessary and even embarrassing if applied to matters of an individual ethic. Niebuhr writes:

> The inferiority of the morality of groups to that of individuals is due in part to the difficulty of establishing a rational social force which is powerful enough to cope with the natural impulses by which society achieves its cohesion; but in part it is merely the revelation of a collective egoism, compounded of the egoistic impulses of individuals which achieve a more vivid expression and a more cumulative effect when they are united in the common impulse than when they express themselves separately and discreetly.[9]

Niebuhr's analysis of collective evils enabled earlier black scholars to have deeper insight into racism as a cultural, institutional, and systematic evil. William Stuart Nelson, Benjamin E. Mays, and others of that generation added Niebuhr's contribution to the insights they had gained from the social gospel in their opposition to racism. Their ethical thought was enriched by their knowledge of black religious experience, their encounter with black people, and their response to racist oppression.

Niebuhr, more than Rauschenbusch, attacked racism in a forthright manner and instructed black leaders concerning the best approach to overcome it. Niebuhr tries to deal realistically with racism as a stubborn collective evil. He understands that blacks must oppose this evil and steer a course between resignation and violent rebellion. He rightly suggests that power must be pitted against power in the black struggle for equality. Niebuhr goes on to say, "It is hopeless for the Negro to expect to complete emancipation from the menial social and economic position into which the white man has forced him, merely by trusting in the moral sense of the white race."[10] He admits that there are individual whites who identify with the cause of racial justice. "The white race in America will not admit the Negro to equal rights if it is not forced to do so."[11]

The full force of Niebuhr's observations on race was never really taken into account until the black community and churches encountered black power. Even such an astute thinker as Martin Luther King Jr., who read Niebuhr both carefully and critically, did not take these insights with great seriousness until he met the advocates of black power in debate and in a leadership struggle. We need to read Niebuhr again as we search for strategic instruments for black liberation while confronting new phases of racism.

The Legacy of Dr. King

It is my contention that any viable position in liberation ethics in this country must take seriously the legacy of Martin Luther King Jr. Thus far the pacesetters in the field have almost ignored his rich contribution, both his thought and his action. James Gustafson has a long chapter on theological ethics in America in one of his books.[12] I have searched in vain to find King's name in those sixty or more pages. The author would swear that he is not a racist, but the document speaks for itself. He is not alone. There are black writers who give King's ethics little if any attention. They are too busy quoting from white ethicists. Since our main task is to come up with some perspective in black liberation ethics, King's work is the more indispensable.

He is the bridge between the older generation of black religious thinkers and the present situation. George Kelsey, Benjamin E. Mays, Mordecai Wyatt Johnson, and Howard Thurman are among those who laid the ethical foundations for King's work. King, in his account of his intellectual development, does not pay adequate respect to black thinkers who prepared the way for him. At the time when he wrote, most black scholars would have claimed respectability by quoting white sources; why should he be the exception? And yet with our new consciousness of the importance of our "roots," we would be remiss if we did not examine his works in the context of the black heritage. Without the black church tradition, there would not have been a Martin Luther King Jr. as we know him. Without a religious experience that steeled black sufferers against hardships and inflamed their consciences against injustices, King would not have emerged as it were from the womb of the black church. Crozer and Boston only refined what he brought with him. Furthermore, his effectiveness as a leader among blacks, even among whites, may be explained only in this way.

King's pilgrimage to nonviolence is well known. It would take too long to restate it here. What King sought was a method to overcome a systemic evil — racism. All of his white teachers had failed to indicate how the ethic of Jesus could deal with overcoming a massive social evil like racism. They had done the exegesis of Scripture and their theological reflection in such an individualistic manner as to render the Christian ethic ineffectual in dealing with a social evil like racism. In the West, Marx and Reinhold Niebuhr have been helpful, but King rejected both on theological grounds — his understanding of God and man.

King describes nonviolent actions as follows: It opposes evil actively. It is a method that is active spiritually. Nonviolence does not seek to humiliate an opponent but cultivates understanding. It attacks the forces of evil rather than the persons who are evildoers because they themselves are victimized by evil. Nonviolence accepts suffering without retaliation. King held that undeserved suffering is redemptive and can educate and transform human nature. Nonviolence avoids internal as well as external violence. One must refuse to hate.[13]

For King, love is the message while nonviolence is the method. He gets love from his understanding of Jesus and the method from Gandhi. He integrates these in his own thought, life, and program. Unfortunately, King accepts the Lutheran version of *agape* of the Lundensians rather than doing his own exegesis. The result is interpreting love as a giving love devoid of the input from *eros* and *philia*. Another weakness is the failure to reconcile justice and power in the theological grounding of his ethics. Unless we observe these deficiencies in King's ethical program, we will not have an adequate ethical perspective for the present and the future. Thus, an affirmative attitude toward King's contribution does not require an uncritical acceptance of his position as a norm for all times to come. The genius of the norm that black Christians have used in the fight against racism has been adaptability to new occasions and new duties.

Here the insights of John Bennett on "middle axioms" prove useful. Our norm is the black experience of the Christian faith. Our goal is human liberation from racism among other social and personal forms of oppression. For us, personal ethics must be subsumed under community ethics. The main focus of black liberation ethics must be social without neglecting a profound concern for personal ethics. We therefore have a norm and a goal. The middle-axiom thesis provides a means whereby the norm is brought in contact with a situation (racist oppression) to lead toward a goal (racial justice/equality).

As we reflect on King's program and seek to update his unusual contribution to ethical thought and action, we must find a way to modify the norm and the goal as we confront a new type of racism initiated by "benign neglect" and culminating in the Bakke case. The new racism is subtle, respectable, highly intellectual, and nationwide. The white conscience no longer exists, or if it does, it does so in a callous, self-righteous, and antagonistic form. The white liberals are tired, and many are now avowed racists. A Latin American theologian could have been describing churches in the United States when he said that in the face of the poverty-stricken masses, the churches are too feeble even to deny their Lord. A colleague said to me recently that white churches are seemingly condemned to hypocrisy on racism.

The picture is dismal, especially when figures are translated into kith and kin and people you care about. But blacks have been in the freedom struggle a long time. In developing a strategy to move forward, black churchmen and churchwomen, black ethicists, and black theologians have a major role. Our inspiration comes from our faith in the Lord of the church and from a communion with black saints and martyrs of the past. They did not fail their generation; we must not fail ours.

Chapter 5

Black Religion

The new emphasis on the black religious experience stems from the so-called black revolution. A turning point occurred with the assassination of Martin Luther King Jr. that signaled the end of hope for integration through nonviolence. The riots in more than one hundred cities and the cry for "black power" inaugurated a new era in race relations in this country. Blacks had lost confidence in America's promises, and they were done with stooping and bowing for freedom and equality.

More and more blacks were talking in terms of liberty or death. Dr. King had said that "no one can ride your back unless you stoop," and he was frequently beaten and imprisoned for his actions. He had preached a doctrine of love and had advocated "turning the other cheek," and his enemies killed him. Young militant blacks concluded that if America is a melting pot, blacks will never melt. After three and a half centuries, only a token number of blacks had been elevated to positions of wealth and influence. The masses were still sunk in the quagmire of illiteracy, poverty, and deprivation. White-skinned immigrants, on the other hand, had been absorbed into the mainstream in this country within two or three generations.

After all the pleading, praying, begging, and marching for freedom during the early sixties, it is not surprising that the tragic death of the apostle of nonviolence triggered a new reaction to an old malady in this country. Black people

Originally published in *Mid-Stream* 22 (July–October 1983): 378–85.

decided to chart a new course. The search for a black heritage began. Since whites of the Euro-American heritage had also banned blacks from the mainstream in religious circles, the quest for a religion of black power, a black messiah, and a black theology was inaugurated. A black caucus appeared in every major religious body in which blacks were a minority.

African Background for Black Religion

"Black religion" refers to Afro-American religion. It is African and it is American in a vital sense. It is African because its historical roots are there, and it is American because it has developed now for several centuries within the American environment. It is my contention that it has remained African in temperament in spite of the tragic history of blacks in this country. All the repressions of slavery and all the indignities of discrimination have not eradicated the essentially African flavor of the black religious experience.

The arguments of E. Franklin Frazier and others notwithstanding, the overwhelming evidence is in favor of "Africanisms" in black religion. Frazier was in many respects a careful scholar. One cannot, for example, read his classic description of the black middle class *The Black Bourgeoisie* without great appreciation for his accuracy and courage. Here Frazier, as a member of the class he described, could give a subjective-objective account of his thesis. If Frazier had gone to the black church more often and had been closer to the life stream of black religion, I am sure his interpretation would have been more positive regarding the survival of the African influence in black religion.

Frazier insisted that it is impossible to establish any continuity between African religious practices and the Negro church in the United States. Since enslavement destroyed the African system of kinship and made the most elementary form of social life, the family, "insecure and precarious," religious myths and cults had no further meaning.[1] Certainly blacks were disoriented by enslavement: "The uprooting of Negroes and the transportation of them to an alien land had a shattering effect upon their lives. In destroying their traditional culture and in breaking up their social organization, slavery deprived them of their accustomed orientation towards the world."[2]

Blacks, it is true, were baptized, but they were taught the Bible in a manner to justify their state of oppression, and they were given an otherworldly understanding of religion. Blacks were expected to accept their lot in this world with the belief that they would be rewarded after death. But for several reasons Frazier does not perceive that blacks never fully accepted this version of Christianity. Since they were not accepted socially into white society, they maintained a separate subculture, part of which was their religious experience. There is an instinctive human rejection of unjust treatment. When blacks heard the Bible read, they provided their own interpretation from their past and present experience. Africans had and still have one of the richest religious backgrounds to be found anywhere; it surely affected their understanding of the Christian faith. Moreover, blacks have non-Western or "oriental" minds; the Bible is an "oriental" book. It is highly possible that blacks understood its original message much better than their teachers did. Above all, the biblical message of freedom from bondage, the theme of the Exodus, had an immediate appeal. These observations become obvious if we look at black religion from the "inside." Frazier stood "outside" and attempted to look in.

In W. E. B. Du Bois's *The Souls of Black Folk,* we get some indication of the survival of the African religious heritage in black religion. Du Bois points out three characteristics of black religion: the preacher, the music, and the frenzy. All of these express a distinctively African temperament. He does not hesitate to assert that the music of black religion had "sprung from the African forests." This music was intensified by the tragic soul life of the slave and became a true expression of the black people's sorrow, despair, and hope. Du Bois sees the poor whites' religion as a plain copy of black religion but a poor reproduction. Their songs, according to Du Bois, are a "debased imitation of Negro melodies made by ears that caught the jungle but not the music, the body but not the soul, of the jubilee songs."[3]

Du Bois described the emotion of black religion:

> The frenzy or "shouting" when the spirit of the Lord passed by, and, seizing the devotee, made him mad with supernatural joy, was the last essential of Negro religion and the one more devoutly believed in than all the rest.... All this is nothing new in the world, but old as religion.... And so firm a hold did it have on the Negro, that many generations firmly believed that without this visible manifestation of God there could be no true communication with the Invisible.[4]

Du Bois is correct, I believe, when he observes: "We must realize that no such institution as the Black church could rear itself without a definite historical foundation."[5]

Paul Radin: The Slaves' Encounter with Reality

Paul Radin raises the question of the value of Christianity for people whose holiest human feelings were being daily outraged, leaving the victims with a sense of degradation and sin. To be sinned against is also sin. The slaves wanted to be cleansed, to be reborn. God was a fixed point, and the slaves needed such a focused point to make sense out of a life of endless shifting. All that God demanded was an unqualified faith. Amid uncertainties and crises, the slaves gave their assent with joy and enthusiasm — even a jubilant hysteria. Through a combination of the natural striving for a unified personality and the need for a fixed God as the center of the world, a new world was forged.

Blacks came from a healthy and virile African strain. They had to be struck down by God. Conversion had to be like a stroke of lightning that entered at the top of the head and emerged from the toes. They had to meet God, be baptized by him personally in the River Jordan, become identified with him. It was not so much that the blacks sought God as God sought the blacks. God literally had to struggle with them, not to persuade them to give up their sins but to force them to express themselves, to fulfill their mission and attain individualization.[6]

Du Bois provides a vivid description of what black religion was like in corporate worship around the turn of the twentieth century:

> And so most striking to me, as I approached the village and the little plain church perched aloft, was the air of intense excitement that possessed that mass of Black folk. A sort of suppressed terror hung in the air and seemed to seize us — a pythian madness, a demoniac possession, that lent terrible reality to song and word. The black and massive form of the preacher swayed and quivered as the words crowded his lips and flew at us in singular eloquence. The people moaned and fluttered, and then the gaunt-cheeked brown woman beside me suddenly leaped straight into the air and shrieked like a lost soul, while round about came a wail and groan and outcry and a scene of human passion such as I have never conceived before.[7]

This emotional characteristic of black religion is the "soul" in black expression uninhibited by the predominant culture. Black religion is not a mild experience; it is more like an acute fever. This tendency toward joyous celebration in worship is not contrived; it is natural. Dialogue between the preacher and the congregation is natural also. The Puritans tried to deculturate Africans. Whereas a "holy dance" was native to Africans, the Puritans forbade it, insisting that dancing is a sin. Blacks "shouted"; they found their natural way of expressing a holy joy. One finds this same joyous celebration today in African religious expression, both Christian and non-Christian. While it is not possible to establish continuity of "soul" in black worship from Africa to the New World beyond any doubt, it is extremely interesting to observe this unusual similarity. (The similarity became obvious to me during a recent field experience in several African countries.)

One observes that African religions have not been given adequate attention in studies of world religions. Part of this omission may be due to a rather negative attitude toward the "dark continent." Many early scholars writing about African religions were not only "Christian" but ex-colonial officials obsessed with a belief in the inherent superiority of the West — its race, culture, and religion — and having devised an evaluative scheme that considered African religion as "heathen," they were not open to a real appreciation of these religions. But beyond this, African social organization is "tribal," and each tribe or group of tribes has a "religion." This means that studying African religions is much like being lost in the forest. Add to the multiplicity of religions the absence of sacred texts and the continuation of a predominantly oral tradition, and one gets a hint of the perplexity that faces any investigator from the West, black or white.

Characteristics of Afro-American Religion

Afro-American investigators have a real advantage if they have stayed in touch with the masses of black folk, for black religion is also based on an oral tradition. Black preachers and black religious scholars are reluctant writers. Our rich religious tradition has, nevertheless, been sustained through a powerful oral tradition that has survived slavery and all oppressions and repressions we have endured in a hostile social environment. A group of black religious scholars who met in Atlanta to seek the basis of what is called a "black theology" concluded that an indigenous theology is implicit in the spirituals and slave songs but is likewise found in the "exhortations of slave preachers and their descendants."[8]

Perception seems to override conception in African and Afro-American religion. In other words, black religion appears to be more existential than metaphysical. Intellection gives way to intuition. This does not imply that black religion is antirational. Feeling is intense, but black religion is more than feeling. It is volitional and cognitive as well as emotive. It is therefore "noetic" in a holistic sense. Knowledge in black religion is personal. It is closer to wisdom than rarified intellection. As the black theologians put it in their Atlanta statement: "It dealt with all the ultimate and violent issues in life and death for a people despised and degraded."[9]

All people need both a temporal and a spatial home. All people need some appreciation of their past as an index to their present and future. Like the Jews, blacks have been scattered and persecuted. But Jews have had a more cohesive religious and group life. They have looked homeward, and even though they have not had a real home, they have had a symbolic home. Blacks need, at least, a symbolic home. Real Africa is a myth to most American blacks, but symbolic Africa is a sheer necessity. The oral history of blacks supports this yearning for a symbolic cultural home, even if white ideological history denies any meaningful continuity between the black experience in Africa and the New World. Rejected by a society that uprooted them for economic reasons from a situation of "at homeness," blacks seek a place to be at home. Alex Haley gives classic expression to this longing in his *Roots*.

Black religion, especially in the black church, has been a haven for black people. The independent black church, invisible before the emancipation and visible after, has been a great preserver of African traditions in Afro-American life.

Even when blacks were forbidden by their captors to worship in the old ways, they still were able to worship in secret.
LeRoi Jones saw clearly the link between black religion in
the New World and African religions: "Many of the 'superstitions' of the Negroes that the whites thought 'charming' were
holdovers from African religions. Even today in many Southern rural areas, strange mixtures of voodoo, or other primarily
African fetish religions, and Christianity exist."[10]

Afro-Americans came from an intensely religious culture
in which religion was a daily concern and not a one-hour-
per-week reaffirmation. Africans could not function as human
beings without religion. White Christians have exploited this
built-in propensity toward religion on the part of blacks. But
while black religion acted as a "pacifier and palliative," it also
"produced a great inner strength among the devout and an
almost inhuman indifference to pain."[11]

Black religion is consoling, but it is also disturbing. It
is at once priestly and prophetic. A religion that is closely
allied with the ruling class in a given society is most likely
to be priestly only. It sanctions the status quo. Priestcraft and
statecraft are one. Whatever is approved by politicians is sanc-
tioned by the priests. The church becomes a department of the
state, and priests become wealthy and privileged. "God and
country" becomes a favorite slogan. The kingdom of God and
the American dream are seen as the same. Very devout Christians sincerely believe that if the kingdom of God comes, it
will be in America.

Black religion will have none of this. As oppressed people,
blacks have developed a sensitivity to injustice and inhumanity
that has become a part of their religious and moral perception.
Their experience of racism has made them keenly aware that
something is radically wrong with America.

Black religion is priestly, however, in its manner of bringing
meaning to the oppressed. Through the agency of black religion, it has been possible to bring purpose into an otherwise
meaningless existence. After a day of worship and fellowship,

blacks have been able to go back into a workaday living hell without being broken.

Western religion informed by Platonic dualism has not been able to put the priestly and prophetic together. It is usually either this-worldly or other-worldly. It is either socially oriented or pietistic. Black religion is a wholesome balance of piety and social concern. Because blacks have been rejected by this society, they look objectively at the society and indeed at the church that has rejected them. The theme of freedom is an ever-present concern for black religion; the Exodus, the prophets of social justice, and Jesus as the great priest-prophet also have great appeal.

Black religion sees life as a whole. In the midst of great suffering, black religionists are able to celebrate life. They are able to affirm the goodness of God and all creation in spite of the realities of oppression at the hands of others. In the context of protest against injustice and the search for meaning, they have found a proper balance between the secular and the sacred. The same holistic view of life is characteristic of African religions. The religious adjustment blacks made in this country was great, but it is also true that their worldview was shaped by the "faith of the fathers."

Howard Thurman, the poet-mystic and philosopher par excellence of the black religious experience, recalls how the spirituals speak of life and death. He points out that black people were nonentities to their oppressors. Their deaths were only a matter of bookkeeping. But in the souls of the blacks, those lives were precious and those deaths had meaning. The oppressors had control of the slaves' lives, but death was out of their control. In a real sense, death was the only thing the blacks could really choose. There was freedom only in dying.

African religion appears to take seriously the afterlife through its family system and reverence for ancestors. The relationship between the living and living dead is at the center of most African religions. Black religion, as I know it, also takes the relationship between the living and the dead seriously. Black hope is rooted in the assurance of a reunion with loved ones and a type of abiding fellowship between the living and the dead.

Black religion has a concern for the here and now but not at the expense of an eternal hope. Black religion affirms this life. It teaches that God's creation is good and that all people should have whatever makes life worth living. Concern for material things, so often condemned in the name of religion, is religious and ethical. We have in black religion a genuine realized eschatology, an eschatology that is inherently ethical. But there is a sense in which the present life is seen from a perspective beyond it. The quality of the present life is enriched because there is an investment in something that transcends it. Thurman has correctly referred to death as an experience within life.

The faith of our black forebears is with us still. There are African traditions in the spiritual strivings of black people. This faith now needs to be articulated against its past, but with a bold consciousness of our needs and aspirations as a people in the present and in the future.

> God of our weary years,
> God of our silent tears,
> Thou who hast brought us
> Thus far on the way;
> Thou who hast by Thy might
> Led us into the light,
> Keep us forever in the path, we pray.
> Lest our feet stray from the places,
> Our God, where we met Thee.
> Lest our hearts, drunk with
> The wine of the world, we forget Thee;
> Shadowed beneath Thy hand
> May we forever stand.[12]

Part 3

Theology and the Church

Chapter 6

A Black Ecclesiology of Involvement

There is a need for a careful theological statement on the black church. The purpose of this theological enterprise is to discern clearly the nature of the black church in order to understand more adequately its mission. The very nature of the black church involves it in the mission of liberation. If the black church is not busy making life more human for black people, it denies its right to be. We need a theology as well as a sociology of the black church. While social history is the context of its theology, social history and theology are not the same. We are in great need of a theology to undergird the worship and service of black Christians in fellowship. One of our greatest mistakes has been to try to outline a different mission for the black church without looking at its theology that stems from black suffering. The result is that black churches are often burning up with piety and emotionalism while those who are concerned about social change operate outside the church, believing it is not in the nature of the black church to be where the action is. We left the ranks of white Christians voluntarily or by the efforts of whites, but we carried their theology and ritual away with us. The black church should have become a revolutionary power for liberation, but with few exceptions it has become a dispenser of spiritual aspirins.

A great deal of the blame falls on those of us who have been trained as theologians and churchmen in the twentieth

Originally published in *Journal of Religious Thought* 32 (spring–summer 1975): 36–46.

century. Being lured on to goals of success as set by the value system of American society, we have been blind to the riches of our religious heritage. Even a latent theology has been present. A treasure chest of theological gems can be found in our folklore, music, art, and literature. We have been lured away by our white teachers to seek religious insights from the Euro-American tradition, which has never given birth to a great religion. Our black fathers had a rich religious heritage in Africa when the Norsemen were living in caves.

There is no existent historical-theological study of the black church by a black theologian. Carter Woodson and W. E. B. Du Bois wrote as laymen, and what they wrote is seriously dated. Mays and Nicholson and the collection by the Nelsens and Yokley are sociological studies. James Cone's brief essay written for the *Encyclopaedia Britannica* (1970) is a good beginning. Cone presents his own theological perspective and at times does not pay enough attention to history. Vincent Harding has little respect for theology and looks more and more like a poet rather than a historian. Yet some of his historical work is very profound, indicating that he may yet contribute to serious historical study of black religion and the black church.

Not only is this historical-theological account of the black church missing, I am not aware that it is forthcoming, though several people have expressed interest and ability regarding the subject through brief installments. Lawrence Jones is an able worker at this task. But the matter is so urgent that the theologian at work on the black experience cannot await these possible studies. This is a matter so urgent that it should have been dealt with yesterday. Sensing the urgency of the matter, I am providing a brief outline of a theology for the black church in its constructive phase with some reflection on history. My real concern here is to show that the very nature of the black church, conceived theologically, leads to acts of liberation from oppression on the part of black people.

Toward a Black Ecclesiology

In a theological study of the church, we will look for representative images of the church that communicate special meaning to black Christians as they seek to understand the nature and mission of the black church. After considering a brief definition of the church, we will embark descriptively on an analysis of three images of the black church: as a chosen people, as a family, and as a body. Throughout we will allude to the social or practical implications of each image or manner of understanding the church, and the final section of the discussion will stress the black church as an instrument for the liberation of black people.

Church is people, not a building. *Ecclesia* in the New Testament means "an assembly of people." *Ecclesia* is used by the Septuagint to translate two Hebrew words *'edhah* and *qahal.* The Revised Standard Version translates *'edhah* as "congregation" and *qahal* as "assembly." Thus, in the Septuagint, a pre-Christian Greek version of the Old Testament used by Greek-speaking Christians, the phrase *"ecclesia* of the Lord" acquires the same theological content as the Hebrew *"qahal* of Yahweh." In both cases we refer to "the people of God." In the Old Testament, reference is to the Israel of the Exodus, while Greek-speaking Christians speak of the reconstituted people of God. But since the people of Israel are the bearers of the divine covenant of promise, the sense of *ecclesia* remains "the people of God."

Ecclesia was first used of the Christian community that was gathered at Jerusalem by the preaching of the apostles (Acts 5:11; 8:1, 3). This community was made up of those who had been baptized and received forgiveness of sins and the gift of the Holy Spirit (Acts 2:37–41). This redeemed community had already received the Spirit of the Messiah. These are the people of God who are heirs of the promise — continuous with the people of the Old Testament (Acts 7:38).

The Apostle Paul saw the local congregation as the embodiment of the universal church, while the whole church is the

universal church. The liturgical assembly is the localization
of the whole people of God. He speaks, for example, of the
church at Corinth rather than "the Corinthian church" (1 Cor
1:2; 2 Cor 1:1). The universal church is locally present. The
Christian community is said to be "the body of Christ" (1 Cor
12:12–27). Or Christ is the head of the church, which is his
body (Eph 1:22; 5:23). The church is "the church of God"
(1 Cor 1:2) or "the church of God in Christ" (1 Thess 2:14).

The church is the assembly of God in Christ. It is a
spirit-filled community. It is not a self-appointed, self-initiated
community. It originates in the redemptive act of God in
Christ and lives through its unity with Christ in his death and
resurrection and through the comfort, guidance, and power of
the Holy Spirit.

The church is more than an organization. It is an organism — a living fellowship. It is more than an institution. It is
an "incendiary fellowship." The church is not a social club. It
is a redeemed community. It is people gathered in the name of
Christ. It is an "event," an extension of the incarnation and
the atonement. The church is the "Israel of God" (Gal 6:16);
a spiritual house (1 Pet 2:5); an elect race, a royal priesthood,
holy nation, people of possession, people of God (1 Pet 2:5,
9–10). The church, however, is not merely a *redeemed* fellowship; it is a *redeeming* fellowship. It is "light," "salt," and
"leaven." It is in the world but not of the world. It is not like
a chameleon — it is like a transformer and it is moved by a
gospel of power.

Reginald H. Fuller states the case thus: "The Church...is
never triumphant, always militant. The Church triumphant
would be identical with the Kingdom of God, and therefore
no longer *ecclesia*."[1]

The words of 1 Peter 2:9–10 are instructive:

But you are a chosen race, a royal priesthood, a dedicated nation, and a people claimed by God for his own,
to proclaim the triumphs of him who has called you out

of darkness into his marvelous light. You are now the people of God, who once were not his people; outside his mercy once, you have now received his mercy. (NEB)

For some strange reason, the oppressed often see themselves as the chosen of God. Perhaps this is basically an attempt to make some sense out of their oppression. Believing that unmerited suffering prepares them for a special mission takes some of the sting out of their misery. If we are aware of the mistakes others have made in the usage of this concept, we may be able to make proper sense and correct use of it. What is our mission as the chosen of God? The understanding of chosenness in black theology must take into consideration the fact that black men have experienced great oppression and that the souls of black men have been purged in the fires of suffering. Our interpretation must exalt the riches of our spiritual past but at the same time promise a better day — the redemption of our future.

The Bible is a favorite book for blacks. It is therefore easy to understand why the theme of the chosen of God is so attractive. Israel of Deutero-Isaiah was a suffering servant of God, a remnant, a saving minority. Jesus was "the Son of Man who suffered." The thrust of this message penetrates to the depths of the black psyche. It is not strange that we should understand our peoplehood and discipleship as the people of God. Biblical imagery and history echo our past and our situation: "You are now the people of God, who once were not his people; outside his mercy once, you have now received his mercy" (1 Pet 2:10 NEB).

A people chosen of God are a people who have entered into a new understanding of their mission in the world. Instead of being victims of suffering, they transmute suffering itself into a victory. If they correctly understand the role of a "suffering servant," they are not led to consider themselves superior or favored before God. They enter into a "stewardship of suffering" with those who "bear the mark of pain." Upon entering into a deeper understanding of how their lives have been purged and purified by unmerited suffering, they become "a saving minority," instruments of God's salvific purpose for all men. Only in this way may black people overcome the danger of assuming the posture of a chosen people and at the same time fulfill the promise and purpose of a "suffering servant of God."

At the same time that we use suffering creatively and redemptively, we must seek to render it unnecessary as a way of life. Not all our suffering has been an "act of God," nor has it been "redemptive suffering." Much of it, too much of it, has resulted from man's inhumanity to man. It is in no way related to an understanding of God's purpose in the world or our mission as a people. This is the cross of black experience that we must get rid of. At the same time, we must seek to transmute suffering into victory; we must strive to transcend suffering that we as individuals and as a people may know the liberty of sons of God *here* as well as *hereafter.* At the same time that we seek reconciliation through our roles as "suffering servants," we are to seek liberation from suffering stemming from being a black in a white man's world. Our Christian understanding of our peoplehood leads us in the search for meaning, service, and protest.

The "family" is one of the few images that still has rich potential for communicating meaning to black people. The search for a wholesome family life has deep roots in our heritage. The movement informed by black consciousness reinforces the place of family life in black experience. It is exceedingly wise for the black theologian to make full use of this imagery in his Christian theological interpretation of the black experience.

The black church, as a social and religious body, has served as a kind of "extended family" for blacks. In a real sense, then, thousands of blacks who have never known real family life have discovered the meaning of real kinship in the black church.

The black theologian has a great opportunity to make constructive use of "the family" as the people of God as expressed through the black church. Thus, we speak of the beloved community, the black church as the family of God.

God is father of the disciples because he is father of Jesus. The disciples are to reproduce the activity of God. The Father confers the kingdom and the Holy Spirit on the disciples. Christians mediate God to others. Christians owe their very spiritual existence to the Father.

Adelphos, "brother," is the universal standard name for Christians. Brotherhood corresponds with the idea of family (Gen 24:4). In ancient Israel, the city-community was a family, and fellow citizens were called brothers; therefore, all Israelites were considered brothers (Exod 2:11). Brotherhood exists where there is "social unity." But "family" in the Christian sense transcends the limits of blood relationship. Jesus claims all humans as brothers (Matt 25:40). The status of a man is entirely changed by membership in the church. We are "no longer...a slave but more than a slave,...a beloved brother" (Philem 1:16).

Jesus places great emphasis on reconciliation and his use of "brother." "If you are offering your gift at the altar, and there remember that your brother has something against you, leave your gift there before the altar and go; first be reconciled to your brother, and then come and offer your gift" (Matt 5:23–24). But at the same time, there can be no Christian reconciliation within the Christian church unless there is liberation from oppression. As one Old Testament prophet put it, God has said: "I hate, I despise your feasts, and I take no delight in your solemn assemblies.... Take away from me the noise of your songs; to the melody of your harps I will not listen. But let justice roll down like waters, and righteousness like an everflowing stream" (Amos 5:21, 23–24).

The black church must proclaim a militant creed. We cannot thrive on "Jesusology" and sentimental love. In our society we face not only the sin of self-glory, the worship of finite white skin instead of the Creator of all life, but we face "conscienceless" power entrenched in the institutions of our society. The black church needs to proclaim more than pie-in-the-sky. We minister to too many people who do not know where the next meal is coming from to expend all of our energy proclaiming heavenly rewards and promises. The black church must be a progressive and active instrument of black liberation in the here and now. It must conceive of salvation in holistic terms. It has the responsibility of ministering to the physical, psychological, social, economic, political — all are basic needs of blacks.

We must, however, have a sound theological understanding of the *nature* of the black church if we are to understand its *mission*. As those who have been a part of a dispersion caused by slavery and subsequent oppression, we have known what it means to be strangers and pilgrims. It is natural, therefore, for the black church to become the "pilgrim church." The white church is in danger of losing its identity in an American civic religion. God and country, White House sermons, the friendship between Billy Graham and Richard Nixon, the support of the American involvement in Vietnam, and many other indicators point to the identity of piety with pragmatism in the white church. We are a people who know the meaning of persecution and suffering. To this prophetic witness we are not only called but chosen — chosen to show the churches that dare not risk the loss of funds, respectability, and social acceptance how to be the church. The black church, which was an "invisible church" during slavery, a haven for homeless suffering masses of black people during all the years of our sojourn in this country, knows what it means to "sing the Lord's song in a strange land."

To bring to focus what we have said thus far concerning the church in the quest for peoplehood, the New Testament image of the church as a body has real possibilities for a black interpretation of the nature of the church. The church is a body — a unity-in-diversity. It is most helpful to a race divided as we are by historical accident to know that in the house of God and as a people we may be brought together again. The image of the body is suggestive of unity-in-diversity (not uniformity that stifles individuality). The image of "body" describes the dependent-independent character of persons-in-community of all human relationships. Each member of the church is important to the group and dependent on the collective body at the same time. In a good family the smallest girl or boy is just as important as the parents. While black nationalism, even Christian black nationalism, preserves the sense of unity, it often doesn't allow for diversity and insists on uniformity, thereby robbing the individual of his or her individuality and talented expression. The church, as a good family, is a fellowship in which every member is "somebody." It has always been a place where blacks who have been "nobodies" through the week have affirmed their dignity as persons. Among members of the body of Christ there is to be togetherness, belongingness, but the dignity of selfhood is to be respected and cultivated. This unity-in-diversity has created the climate for the development of black leaders. There is to be mutual respect, appreciation for all gifts and talents, and full cooperation toward the realization of the true ends of the church. It is not an accident that so many blacks who have excelled in secular vocations came out of the black church. It is interesting that so many sons and daughters of ministers, who have not chosen a religious vocation, get involved in programs designed to liberate black people.

The need for a theology of the black church is not obvious to everyone. Many would like to discuss the *mission* of this church without dwelling on its *nature*. My reason for approaching the black church in the manner that I have is because what it is determines what it does and what it can do to liberate black people. The church needs to see the relation between its worship and its service. In our heritage of oppression, we have not been afforded the luxury of separating faith from life. But we have not interpreted in a formal manner the theological basis for our church life. We have rather been influenced by white interpreters of the faith who have a divided mind of sacred versus secular. We left the white churches for nontheological reasons. Many blacks believe they must be indifferent to theology and even leave the church if they really want to get involved in acts of black liberation. They do not see how the theological understanding of faith relates to the problems of the here and now. The black church out of sheer necessity is a militant church, and there is no conflict between faith and protest. Entering to worship and departing to serve are one religious affirmation.

Furthermore, we need to understand that the church is not an organization or institution alongside other institutions. The moment the church becomes just another agency, it loses its redemptive power in the world. Other organizations can easily out-organize and out-perform the church as social technicians and engineers. The church is an organism, a living fellowship. It is "the house that love built." It is a spiritual body and not merely a social club. Whenever the church loses its theological foundation, it loses the power for mission in the world. Because the church majors in faith, hope and love and cultivates deep personal relationships among individuals and groups, it is a center of great personal and collective power and influence. Even though it is limited in what it can do in a material sense, it is able to get people to seek help where it may best be found. As a powerful assembly of people, the church has a lot of muscle to move institutions to humanize their programs and goals. Thus, the mission, power, and influence of the church is based on a theological understanding of its nature. A young man who leaves the ministry to serve elsewhere because the church isn't doing anything may not understand its nature and therefore cannot participate in its mission.

The Black Church as a Socializing Agent

The Black Church and Health

There is a relationship between faith and healing. There is an undeniable connection between the will to live and the experience of health and wholeness. The black church has always been a survival fellowship. Viktor Frankl states as a basic principle of his logotherapy, "If you have a 'why' to go on living you can endure almost any 'how.'"

As a pastor, I sat by the bedside of a critically ill member of my church, seeking to bring assurance to a believer of many years. I recall the words of the surgeon, a deeply religious man, spoken to me just before I entered the sickroom. He said, "I have done my level best; I have used all the skill and knowledge available to me. If she lives, it will be because of her faith in God and her faith in life itself. And this is where you come in."

Believe it or not, the church has a ministry to all those who are in the helping professions. Who would believe that a psychiatrist needs to be ministered to as well as his clients? Those who move daily in the midst of poverty, mental illness, disease, and all manner of troubles need an anchoring and consoling faith to keep them strong and steadfast in their service. Some time ago I visited a student in a mental hospital. After talking with the patient, I had a brief visit with his therapist. As I took my leave, the psychiatrist offered to show me down to the street floor. It turned out that the psychiatrist, a black woman, was a deeply troubled person who had turned away from her childhood faith and had quit going to church. Now she felt the need for the faith and fellowship she had lost. Her own life was empty, and she was finding her knowledge and skill inadequate to face the problems of others without a restoral of this faith and meaning in her life.

We could go on with similar illustrations, but our purpose here is to indicate the role of the church as a socializing agent.

I am not seeking to win converts to the faith or to the ministry but to indicate the possibilities of the black church as an ally in dealing with serious problems in the black community as well as attacking the injustices in the larger society. As we bring to a close our brief discussion on the black church and health, let us remember the close affinity between healing and religion in the entire African and Afro-American religious heritage. The medicine man was the forerunner of the black pastor. Most nativistic religions in Africa in the postcolonial period have combined salvation and healing. Furthermore, the church, as a gathering of people, may easily become a referral center for professional health services. The fact is that many who need health services need to be encouraged to seek them. In addition, churches may provide information and transportation and may even assist persons in securing funds to procure health services.

The Black Church and Political Economy

The black church has unusual ability to assemble large numbers of black people. Black congregations own large buildings that double as places of worship and community centers where under black leadership we have privacy to "take care of business." The black church is potentially the most powerful institution manned by black people.

Black churches can influence masses of blacks to use the ballot. Though churches should not make blanket endorsement of parties and candidates, they have the responsibility to encourage responsible citizens. We cannot afford to endorse anything but "issues." For a long time black churches followed the Republican party, the party of the emancipation, until it became clear that this was the party of the "haves," the rich and the powerful. We also discovered that Lincoln fought the Civil War to save the Union and not because he loved the black and the poor. We then turned to the Democrats because they appeared to have more of a mass following, but here too we must insist on a black agenda. One party ignores us and the other refuses to take us seriously. If the black congregations across this land rallied around the issues that affect the life of the black masses, the political climate would be more favorable for us. If we were a lobbying church, if we worked hand in glove with the Black Caucus, if we put pressure on local politicians and national politicians from our area, a politician could not survive without our support. We could form ad hoc coalitions with others of goodwill and humanize institutions that control the destiny of the black and the poor throughout this nation.

On the economic front, the black church has similar power. We own a lot of real estate. We control a lot of funds. But much of our money goes out of our communities and ends up in white banks and institutions. We need to use our collective economic strength through the church to improve the conditions in the black community. What we need is a new value system, a different standard of success than that of the majority society. Our priorities must be different, and we must remember that we cannot be saved one by one but as a people. As long as we place emphasis on consumption rather than saving and investment, we cannot do this. Black churches will remain part of the problem rather than its solution as long as they place their emphasis upon buildings rather than social welfare programs. Reverend Leon Sullivan's Opportunities Industrialization Center, which has trained thousands of unemployed and unemployable people, illustrates what black churches can do in the economic field.

The Black Church and Black Culture

One of the strongest assets the black church has is its role as the preserver of black culture. Black religion as expressed through black worship has the means to make use of a wide spectrum of the components of the black heritage. Through

the worshiping church supported by teaching and action programs, the black church can express and transmit much of the
black cultural heritage. In sermon, song, and artistic expression, we can gain a real appreciation for the riches of our
cultural heritage.

As John Vandercook has well said in his *Tom-Tom:* "A race
is like a man. Until it uses its own talents, takes pride in its
own history, and loves its own memories, it can never fulfill
itself completely."[2]

If, then, through the black church as a chosen people, as a
family, and as a body, we are able to find the identity, pride,
and purpose needed to recover our peoplehood, we may then
know the black church as a powerful socializing agent making life more human for the black and the poor throughout
this land.

Chapter 7

The Status of Black Catholics

All African Americans live in the shadow of slavery. Indeed, slavery was the American holocaust, and it is impossible to fully understand race relations in the United States without a consideration of what this tragic institution did to the psyche and conscience of both blacks and whites.

A Historical Perspective

Blacks had begun to convert to the Catholic faith by the time of the Civil War. Benjamin J. Blied has provided a careful discussion on Catholics and the Civil War in which he asserts that Catholics were divided over the institution of slavery. Few were radical abolitionists, but the Catholic leadership reflected very much the division in the country between North and South. In some cases Catholic laypersons, especially journalists, overcame the provincial outlook and fully supported the abolitionist view.[1]

On the whole, Catholics, like other white Christians, were not morally outraged over black slavery. The Civil War was more about politics than the evil of human bondage. The North was usually academic in regard to slavery; the South savored the economic benefits of slavery. For example, some Northerners argued that it would be cruel to free the slaves. Slaves were like children in need of parental protection. No loving parent

Originally published in *Journal of Religious Thought* 48 (summer–fall 1991): 73–78.

would turn children out into the world at a tender age, they reasoned. The abolitionists were viewed as fanatics, agnostics, and irrational persons. Besides, some masters were good to their slaves, especially those who instructed them in Christian belief and practice. No one inquired of the slaves what it was like to be a slave or if they desired to be free. For their testimony, one needs to note the slave insurrections and read some definitive slave narratives, such as Frederick Douglass's *Narrative of the Life of an American Slave.*[2]

Catholics seemed to find it possible to live with the regional ethos in whatever section of the nation they resided. They did not question the local pattern in race relations. They did provide worship, education, and services, but they did so in keeping with the acceptable custom in each locale. In the South, Catholics were in the minority except in Mississippi and Louisiana, where there was a sizable population of Catholics. Again, even in the North, many Catholics were immigrant groups unsure of their own status, fighting for their group survival. The struggle of blacks emerging from slavery and burdened by discrimination was not high on their agenda.

The Catholic church itself is somewhat abnormal in the South. Once in a course I taught on world religions, a white student from the South admitted that he did not know that Roman Catholics were Christians. Those whites who have been brought up in the Anglo-Saxon Protestant tradition have had to struggle with their lack of knowledge concerning Roman Catholics. One only needs to recall that the Ku Klux Klan targeted not only blacks but also Catholics and Jews.

Black Catholics have been nurtured primarily in the Anglo-Saxon Protestant tradition; slaves frequently became Baptist and Methodist during slavery. It is not easy for blacks to be at home in the Catholic church. In doctrine and liturgy, it is strange and distant. Blacks join Catholic congregations more often as a matter of class status than religious commitment. This is likewise true of black membership in the Episcopal or Presbyterian denomination.

The Inevitability of Father Stallings

Father Stallings's stepping upon the stage of current events was logical and inevitable. Black Catholics have been patient and long-suffering, and Stallings is correct in much that he says frankly and forthrightly; more has to be done than wait. In the launching the Imani Temple, one is reminded of Martin Luther King's impatience in his *Why We Can't Wait!*

Being at the first mass of Father Stallings's Imani Temple was a moving experience. My wife and I attended this event on the campus of the Howard University Law School. Since the law school was formerly a Roman Catholic school, it has a large chapel and a smaller chapel. Both were full and the crowd overflowed on the campus outside. A sound system was set up to accommodate all the worshipers.

The weather was hot and there was no air conditioning. Hundreds of black people crowded into the main chapel, making the situation very uncomfortable. Amid flashing cameras, African dancing, and shouts of "Amen!" Stallings inaugurated his new movement. The pulpit party was ecumenical, including representatives of the Islamic community. There was a sense of black unity and black history in the making. Stallings's message was emotional, courageous, and powerful. The celebration lasted for more than three hours, but few were in a hurry to leave. Stallings seemed to have the right message, for the right audience, at the right time. The inevitable was happening.

Black Catholics have long sensed a powerlessness in a powerful church. They have also wanted what has been described as a black rite to express black spirituality and culture in worship. All this and more was embodied in Stallings and the opening of the Imani Temple.

A number of black bishops have been appointed since the 1970s—I am aware of thirteen—though I do not know how many have the full authority of bishop. Moreno of Atlanta, as an archbishop, is the highest ranking. Stallings did not receive

strong endorsement from any of these bishops.[3] On the other
hand, Cardinal John J. O'Connor's statement to black Catholics
was more forceful than anything I have read by a black bishop.[4]
The black bishops have limited their statement mainly to the
need for an African American rite. It is reported that the black
Roman Catholic bishops have initiated a preliminary study
to see if there is a felt need for such a rite. Auxiliary Bishop
John Ricard of Baltimore has made a statement outlining the
difficulties of a black rite. He chairs the United States Bishops' Committee on Black Catholics. Bishop Ricard is correct,
I believe, in pointing to the many problems that would arise if
such a rite were established. He insists there would be problems
of liturgy, canon law, and other disciplines.[5] This immediately
points to the racism inherent in the Roman Catholic church.
Blacks have not been prepared, as theologians, to participate
in preparing a rite for themselves. The spokesperson on this
matter is Monsignor Frederick McManus of Catholic University. Stallings has already pointed to Catholic University, under
the leadership of Cardinal Hickey, as a racist institution. His
statistics are compellingly accurate.

Bishops, of whatever race or denomination, are cautious
and conservative. They have an investment in the stability of
the institution as well as their own authority. This is the reason
black Catholics must depend on those who have some distance from the institutional power structure to champion their
cause. In the absence of theologians (e.g., Küng, Boff, Curran),
they must rely on priests such as Stallings and Brother Joseph
Davis of the Josephites.

Necessity of a Black Catholic Theology

While black Catholics search for identity in a powerful white
church, black priests are at the crossroads. They are engaged
in soul searching regarding their roles in the Catholic church
and parish. Priests and nuns, above all, must find their place as

those who are both Catholic and authentically black in order to be effective in their ministry.[6]

The Catholic church finds itself short on black leadership at a time when black parishioners are demanding a greater leadership presence. There is a shortage of qualified new clergy in all Christian bodies. Roman Catholics are hit especially hard by this shortage.[7] Racism along with the celibacy requirement for priests has caused the ranks of black Catholic priests to be seriously depleted.

Even those black priests who are still active are seriously considering their role in the church. In a recent newspaper article, Rev. Edward Branch, an assistant pastor of St. Augustine's, a historic black congregation in Washington, recalls an event that occurred some fifteen years ago from the time of writing.[8] As a parish priest, Father Branch was asked by community organizers to allow Angela Davis to speak in his church. Branch was inclined to open his church to this event. The local archbishop had just signed a letter advocating the use of church property for discussions of social justice. The archbishop, however, disagreed with Father Branch and objected to the Davis event. Protests followed at the archbishop's house and at the cathedral. A discussion over authority and activism ensued between Branch and the archbishop. Branch reminded the archbishop that Davis was a Catholic as well as a Marxist and urged him to show his unity with black parishioners. The archbishop expressed sympathy for the cause but canceled the meeting. The meeting was eventually held at a black Congregational church whose minister was a liberal white.

The Catholic ministry is also deprived of the contributions of gifted and learned black women. Since women cannot be ordained as priests, they are unable to find full expression as ministers or theologians. Some of the best minds among black Catholics are those of black women. Several of them now possess Ph.D.'s in theology and other disciplines. They are outstanding scholars and teach in academic centers around the nation. Black women share the concerns of white women, but they are burdened by both racism and sexism.

During the time that Father Edward K. Braxton completed his doctoral studies in Belgium, black Catholics invested much hope in his return. They expected that Braxton would develop a program of black theology for black Catholics that would parallel the Protestant program. Thus far he has not done so. His perspective is not sufficiently informed by black history and culture to ever perform this role. He is enchanted with metaphysics and does not see that the black heritage has relevance for what he calls the "classic" tradition in theology.[9] This is his choice, and he has every right to his own outlook. Unfortunately, black Catholics are left without a theological advocate.

James Cone has presented his appraisal of this situation and has examined the situation of black Catholics extensively in his book *Speaking the Truth.* Cone believes that creative theology by black Catholics is virtually impossible. There is little possibility that such a project would assume a critical or prophetic task: "Theology should interpret the truth of the Gospel for the times in which we live so that it has continuity with the past but also challenges and exposes the present contradictions, thereby empowering the oppressed to make a new future for themselves."[10]

I have had the privilege of knowing and teaching black priests who could have developed into outstanding Roman Catholic theologians. They had the intellectual ability and the sensitivity to the black heritage to develop a black Roman Catholic theology. They have become effective priests to black congregations, but they were not encouraged to become theologians. This is an area in which leadership needs to be developed.

After Stallings: What About the Future?

Most Roman Catholic leaders who have responded to Stallings have asked him not to leave the church. Many church leaders have also admitted that there is much racism in the church — this is encouraging. Cardinal Hickey, who has suspended Stallings from functioning as a priest, has not yet excommunicated him. In a moving statement, Hickey invited Stallings "back home."[11]

The Pontifical Commission Iustitia et Pax released a comprehensive twenty-two page statement on racism.[12] It is impressive in its global history and sociology. The remarks about racism in the United States and South Africa are candid, though much too brief. There is little in the theological ethics section that any devout Christian can question. It makes concrete suggestions as to how racism may be addressed in ministry, education, and social service. The report, however, suffers from a few weaknesses: (1) Its observations on racism are too sweeping and general. They are not sufficiently culture-specific. (2) Racism is summarily mixed with ethnocentricity. The concern for minorities is multicultural. This makes the analysis too abstract and simplistic. (3) It is obviously written by men. Sexism as a form of oppression merits more consideration, especially since it is so general and global. If the document discusses everyone else who is hurting, why not women? And (4) it obviously did not express the pain of the victims of racism. They were not on the commission. As we have seen, black Catholics lack theological representatives. Without such representation there can be no adequate treatment of the experience of racism in the American Catholic church. Thus, the very attempt to address racism is blunted by the racism that has prevented blacks from having their voice in this powerful universal church.

Many devout black Catholics have decided that they cannot be black and Catholic, and they are returning to their roots. Others are disturbed regarding their powerlessness in a church of great power. Some two million black Catholics deserve to be heard. The development of an African American rite would no doubt be an effective step forward. But that will not be enough. Racism must be uprooted "root and branch" in all aspects of Roman Catholic life. Blacks must share in decision-making at the highest levels of church authority. For instance, black Catholics need more full bishops, archbishops, and even cardinals. Many third world Catholics are thus represented. Why not African Americans? They must have their representative theologians to contextualize the faith for black people against the background of their history and culture. Stallings has lifted the aspirations of African American Catholics, and there should be no turning back.

Part 4

Theology and African Consciousness

Chapter 8

African Religion and Social Consciousness

My several years of labor in the history of religions have been an asset to this brief investigation into African religion and social consciousness. I have even discovered that there are "theologians" of the traditional African religions as well as African Christian scholars who are "Africanizing" Christianity. Thus, even if my hearers are left with an "inclusive conclusion," I have been greatly rewarded for my efforts. What I have discovered is the measure of my ignorance and the dimensions of my subject. It is hoped that those who listen will share this "Socratic wisdom" and together with me begin the long, hard search for enlightenment.

African religion has this in common with black religion: It has been greatly neglected by Western scholarship. White scholars, with few exceptions, have applied a "colonial" mentality to African studies. Studies resulting from this subordination-superordination syndrome have not yielded the authentic information we need concerning African peoples and their religions. For example, some scholars upon finding traces of advanced civilization in various parts of tropical Africa have explained these finds by foreign influences on Africa. They refuse to accept them as internal developments because of the preconception of Africa as "the dark continent," which they connect with heathenism or primitivism in the worst sense of these terms.

Originally published in *Journal of Religious Thought* 28 (fall–winter 1971): 95–111.

In this country at least, African studies will improve as a result of black consciousness. To the extent that the black scholar associates his own cultural revival with his African heritage, he will promote authentic African studies. My own investigations into the religions of man, together with an examination of numerous sources, has led me to the conclusion that African religions have suffered a "benign neglect" in this field. The better textbooks on world religions treat African religions in the preliminary sections along with all so-called primitive religions and then move on to the "great religions." I have not found a text in the field that provides an adequate treatment of African religions. One has to turn to special volumes for this material. A publisher recently requested my opinion on a proposed text in world religions that was in this same tradition. My negative reaction to the text was decisive. The study of African religions may be only a by-product of pan-African studies, but since religion is the most cohesive subject associated with this movement, the new knowledge of African religions will be considerable.

In recent years there has been an intense interest in Asian religions. My earlier studies were almost exclusively in the religions of South Asia and the Far East. Later I became interested in Islam both in South Asia and the Middle East. The black cultural revival, especially my concern for the role of religious experience in it, led me to Afro-Arab Islam and then to the religions of tropical Africa. The task of writing a black theology has caused me to read history backwards in search of the faith of my fathers.

One of the most wholesome trends recently has been the emergence of African interpreters of African religions. I have long recognized the richness of the inside interpretation of a religion by a "believer-scholar." The Reverend John S. Mbiti is an African theologian who was trained in this country and in England. Though a Christian theologian, he is likewise a historian of religion. Because he is in touch with the African religious experience and at the same time acquainted with English, French, and German sources, he is able to communicate well with those of us who have a Westernized understanding of religious knowledge. Several of Mbiti's observations are noteworthy. I will enumerate some of these here, though I have arrived at a similar conclusion independently as I have studied other non-Western religions and cultures.

During the nineteenth century, African religions were described by European and American missionaries and by students of anthropology, sociology, and comparative religion. But the academic atmosphere was filled with the theory of evolution, which was applied in many fields of study. The theory of evolution therefore colors many descriptions, interpretations, and explanations of African religions.

It was believed that Africa borrowed many of its beliefs, characteristics, and foods from the outside. All types of theories developed to explain how various religious traits reached Africans from the Middle East or Europe. There is evidence that Africa has always had contact with the outside world, but these contacts were made on a "give and take" basis.[1]

These earlier theories are inadequate for a treatment of traditional African religions. The evolutionary theories took the position that monotheistic religions are superior to polytheistic religions. Christianity, Judaism, and Islam are monotheistic religions. They are for this reason higher on the scale of evolution than traditional African religions which were classified as polytheistic or animistic. This theory was lifted up by E. B. Taylor in his *Primitive Culture*. African religions include belief in spiritual beings (God, spirits, and divinities), but these elements of religion are found in all religions. The "high god" of most African religions is likewise a phenomenon to reckon with. It is obvious that this evolutionary approach that placed African religions at the bottom is derogatory and prejudicial.[2] It is little wonder that some scholars have abandoned the quest for "origins" and turned to "description."

Again "redemptive" religions are played over against "primitive" religions. Christianity, Judaism, and Islam are said to be redemptive religions, whereas African religions are classified as primitive religions. Even so-called "morality religions" such as Shintoism and Confucianism were exalted above African religions. By "primitive," many Western writers meant "savage," even though the Latin root *primus* does not carry a bad connotation. Thus, this approach reflected a lack of respect and carried with it derogatory implications. To hold such a superficial attitude toward African religions is to miss the fact that some traditional African religions are extremely rich and complex. Several of these religions contain beliefs and practices that shed light on the study of all religions of the world.[3]

Herbert Spencer, in his *Principles of Sociology,* describes his understanding of ancestor worship among those he calls "savages." He asserts that these peoples associated the spirits of the dead with certain objects, and in order to keep within the favor of these ancestors, they made sacrifices to them. Spencer's speculation set the stage for several writers who associated this meaning of ancestor worship with almost everything Africans do in religious ceremonies. Thus, African religions are spoken of primarily as ancestor worship. We know that the departed occupy a significant place in African religiosity, but Africans do not worship their ancestors. The departed, that is, parents, brothers, sisters, and children, form part of the extended family. They must be kept in touch with their surviving relatives. A fellowship exists between the departed and the surviving relatives. Libation and the giving of food to the departed are tokens of fellowship, hospitality, and respect. What is offered is a symbol of family continuity and contact. The relation between members of the family goes deeper than these tokens or symbols.[4]

Magic has sometimes been identified with religion by some students of African religions. This too is misleading. The evolutionists held that magic is the mother of religion. This

general position was exalted by several distinguished scholars, including E. Durkheim, J. Frazer, B. Malinowski, and
W. Schmidt. Magic is said to have evolved before religion as a
means to control the unseen world. When man failed to control natural objects by means of magic, he was led to a belief
in God as the source of all power. Africans had not evolved
to the point of separating religion from magic. Some went
so far as to assert that Africans have no religion at all and
only magic. Magic is part of the religious background among
Africans. Some ceremonies, for example, rainmaking and the
preventing of epidemics, may be said to be religious and magical at once. Magic does belong to the "religious mentality"
of Africans. But religion is not magic and magic is not religion. Religion is greater than magic and to be unaware of
this is to miss a deep understanding of African religions.[5] Jack
Mendelsohn, a sympathetic Westerner, has made this remark:

> It is altogether too easy for modern Americans and Euro-
> peans to overlook the uses of magic in their own past
> and present, and to forget that, lacking other satisfying
> explanations and means of control, magic has a most
> appealing inner logic and spiritual authority. Its base is
> an instinctive reaction of man to the mysterious and
> often malignant behavior of the Nature of which he is a
> part. He sees the results of the activities he cannot under-
> stand stem from unseen beings, and from this he develops
> an entire spiritual universe.[6]

Other terms, such as dynamism, totemism, and fetishism,
also are used to describe the character of African religions.
It is obvious that these words point to some vital aspect of
African religions. The plea here is for objectivity, empathy, and
intellectual honesty in the scholarly investigation of African
religions. For outsiders the mood should be one of listening,
sitting down with the facts, and suspending judgment (especially value judgment) until the evidence is weighed. Thus, I
basically agree with Mbiti when he concludes:

African religions...have been subject to a great deal of misinterpretation, misrepresentation and misunderstanding. They have been despised, mocked and dismissed as primitive and underdeveloped. One needs only to look at the earlier titles and accounts to see the derogatory language used, prejudiced descriptions given and false judgments passed upon these religions. In missionary circles they have been condemned as superstition, satanic, devilish and hellish. In spite of all these attacks, traditional religions have survived; they dominate the background of African peoples, and must be reckoned with in the middle of modern changes.[7]

We turn now to more recent studies. A new approach to African religion is represented by Placide Tempels's *Bantu Philosophy,* Janheinz Jahn's *Muntu,* and John V. Taylor's *Primal Vision.* The first appeared in French and English, the second in German and English, and the third in English.

According to Tempels, primitive peoples have a concrete conception of being and of the universe. This ontology gives a special character to beliefs and religious practices and to language, institutions, and customs. What Tempels calls "vital force" is the "essence of being." Force is being and being is force. His philosophy of force is the clue to the thought, action, and worship of Africans.[8]

Tempels opens the way to a more sympathetic study of African religions. As a missionary among the Baluba of the Bantu people, he addresses fellow colonialists with a desire to inform them from his many years among this one people. There is a real question as to whether Tempels's "vital force" may be applied broadly to all African religions, but his sympathy and positive attitude are refreshing and point us in the right direction.[9]

Jahn treats what he calls "neo-African cultures." He is primarily interested in Africa south of the Sahara, "Black Africa." Jahn states his goals thus: "We speak in this book...

not about 'savages,' 'primitives,' 'heathens' or 'Negroes,' but about Africans and Afro-Americans, who are neither angels nor devils but people."[10]

It is difficult for European authors to accept the authenticity of real African culture. A prime example of the usual European attitude toward African culture is found, according to Jahn, in Malinowski's *Theory of Cultural Change.* What we have in Africa is a hybrid culture. The new forms are neither African nor European. The word "slokian" is illustrative of this type of cultural change. Slokian, a cocktail of alcohol, calcium carbide, and tobacco that is drunk in the slums of Johannesburg, is something new, belonging neither to Europe nor to Africa. It resulted from African slums and Boer Puritan loathing of African beer. Police regulations that forbade beer led the Africans to invent a drink that could be made and stored in small quantities, that was easy to hide, that could be matured in a few hours, and that could have its alcohol effect quickly.

According to Malinowski, all new objects, facts, and forms of life in Africa are the result of European pressure and African resistance. Even African nationalism recognizes European superiority. When Africans find discrimination, they fall back on their own systems of belief, value, and feeling.[11]

Jahn rejects Malinowski's functional theory of cultural change. *Muntu* is a significant philosophical category. It includes God, spirits, the departed, human beings, and some trees. These constitute a "force" endowed with intelligence. According to Jahn, three other important categories are important as well. First is *Kintu,* or all the forces that do not act on their own but under the direction of *Muntu.* Examples include plants, animals, and minerals. Second, *Hantu* is the category of time and space. Third, *Kuntu* is "modality," that is, beauty and laughter. Jahn is influenced by Tempels's concept of "force." All of these categories or forces are represented by the linguistic stem *NTU,* "the universal force." *NTU* is Being itself — it is the force in which Being and beings coalesce. *NTU* expresses, not the effect of these forces, but their being.[12]

Once again Jahn may not be exact in his conclusions. He appears so enthusiastic about African religion and philosophies that he may have overstated his case. But he does make the point that there is a real African culture that exists in its own right and that has great value and deserves to be taken seriously and studied accordingly.

John V. Taylor is concerned with "the Christian presence" in Africa. In his *Primal Vision,* he attempts to describe "the primal world" for European readers and seeks to penetrate African traditional religion with a Christian theological viewpoint. While he provides a good survey of the whole continent, at times he is carried away by what he found in Africa to the extent that he is too sympathetic and uncritical. African traditional religion is said to be so sacred, holy, pure, and clean that all pollution comes from outside — from Christianity, westernization, urbanization, and technology. He makes a clear distinction between "we" (Europeans) and "them" (Africans) and is concerned about what we can learn from them. *The Primal Vision* points the way to what Mbiti refers to as "Africanizing" Christianity.[13] Others writing with this type of perception are Jack Mendelsohn, *God, Allah and Ju Ju,*[14] and Noel Q. King, *Religions of Africa.*[15]

Another approach, while remaining open to truth, attempts to provide a more systematic understanding of traditional African beliefs. Representative authors with this outlook include E. G. Parrinder, *African Traditional Religion* (1954); H. Deschamps, *Les religion de l'Afrique noire* (1960); and E. Dammann, *Die Religionen Afrikas* (1963). Parrinder does a sympathetic but critical job handling materials from many parts of Africa. His is a noteworthy introduction. Deschamps is limited to western Africa and for the most part to French-speaking countries. As an anthropologist, his treatment is limited in the full understanding of religion. Dammann's work makes use of English, French, and German sources. It is valuable for its comprehensiveness and description.

There also are intense studies that concentrate on the religion of individual peoples. These studies treat the religion in question both in depth and in relation to the total situation of the people concerned. Here we may mention two representative classical anthropological studies. One is by E. E. Evans-Pritchard, *Nuer Religion* (1956), and the other is G. Lienhardt's *Divinity and Experiences: The Religion of the Dinka* (1961). Evans-Pritchard's study resulted from a long study of the Nuer people. The writer lived with them, learned their language, and participated in their activities as much as possible. As a participant-observer, he describes Nuer religion from the inside. While he uses the tools of a skilled anthropologist, he attempts to look at the religion through the eyes of a Nuer believer. The result is a profound insight into the Nuer religion with its deep conception of God as Spirit. Lienhardt's study yields a similar understanding of Dinka religion. This religion lifts up the theme of the personal encounter between God and men. The Dinka see the world of the spirit beings as converging in human experience. The real value of these studies is that they place traditional African religion in the context of Africans' sociological and cultural environment. Without studies of this type, it is impossible to appreciate or understand any religion whatsoever.

The most invaluable contribution to traditional African religious studies is that being provided by African scholars themselves. There is no substitute for a study by a good African scholar who takes a given religion (especially that of his own tribe) and describes it and interprets it in the light of African experience and understanding. The knowledge he has of his people, and often of the religion as a believer, is invaluable. Studies by J. B. Danquah, *The Akan Doctrine of God* (1944) and E. B. Idowu, *Olodumare: God in Yoruba Belief* (1962) are representative. One is reminded of the trilogy on Asian religions (Hinduism, Islam, and Buddhism) edited by

Kenneth Morgan.[16] In these volumes choice Asian scholars use convictional language in describing their own traditional faith. Postcolonial traditional African theologians are now making a similar contribution. Christian Gaba, who as an African himself is writing about African religions, refers to this scholarly process as auto-ethnography. Gaba, of the University of Ghana, has described both the promise and dangers of this role so well that I quote at length from him here:

> The best qualified person then is an auto-ethnographer, that is, a person born and bred in the general surroundings of the area of the research. In short, the student must have been nurtured in the culture of which the religions form a part.... Apart from the language advantage, the auto-ethnographer provides security of a kind for his informants. The people give out relevant information freely....
>
> On the other hand to be the recorder of one's own culture does not go without its dangers. The inquirer may be expected by his informants to know certain facts which they consider basic.... Then — and this is most dangerous — he may out of sympathy and indiscriminate nationalism be tempted to present local values out of their true perspective.[17]

Insofar as the "mark of oppression" that follows colonialism in Africa is similar to the experiences of Afro-Americans under slavery and discrimination, Africans may miss the richness of their own religious heritage if they have been deculturated by whites. Some Africans see their own heritage as inferior through European eyes and through travel, study, and brainwashing. While a nationalistic consciousness has the disadvantage of giving too much credence to one's own tradition, the viewing of one's own culture through the eyes of a self-styled superior culture or religion leads one to see too little good or richness in one's own religion and culture. Africans and Afro-Americans must seek to steer clear of both dangers.

By now the listener or reader will have begun to appreciate the enormous expanse of this study of African religions, to say nothing of the complexity of the subject. Mbiti is not very encouraging when he dares to remind us that there are about one thousand African peoples (tribes), and that each has its own religious system. But we are compelled to forge ahead in our endeavor to understand the African religious mind. Without such an understanding, we cannot understand much of Africa or Africans. Mbiti observes:

> These religions are a reality which calls for academic scrutiny and which must be reckoned with in modern fields of life like economics, politics, education, and Christian or Muslim work.... Religion is the strongest element in traditional background, and exerts probably the greatest influence upon the thinking and living of the people concerned.[18]

It would be a serious mistake to conclude that there is an abundance of knowledge concerning African religion even on the part of scholars well versed in world religions. We saw earlier that most scholars who have been our guides in comparative religion (now history of religion) have either ignored African religions or treated them as an elementary form of religious life under "animism" or "primitive" religion. Mircea Eliade, by making the study of "primitivism" a clue to all religious knowledge, has taken African mythology and symbolism seriously. While this phenomenological approach is helpful, we need now to advance our appreciation of African religions much further. Even those who have included African religions as a special concern among other religions, as in the case of the fine work by Helmer Ringgren and Åke V. Ström entitled *Religions of Mankind,* there is still the Western bias of lifting Egyptian religions out of the African setting as a part of Mediterranean religious studies. This trend continues in the face of our knowledge of the intercommunication between Egypt and the rest of Africa. Frank Snowden, professor of

classics at Howard University, has sought to correct the assertion that Africans borrowed everything worthy from outside
not only by lifting up their contribution within but by pointing to their share in Greco-Roman civilization as well. In his
Blacks in Antiquity, Snowden is speaking of "Ethiopians" in
the Greco-Roman experience. "Ethiopian" is a pan-African
term as used here.

Yosef ben-Jochannan, in his *African Origins of the Major
Western Religions,* makes an extreme claim for African religions as being original. While I appreciate his zeal to place
African religions where they belong within the study of the
religions of mankind, it is rather late and unwise to be preoccupied with "origins." Most respectable scholars have wisely
turned to a description and analysis of any religion studied.
This is all I expect for African religions. When there is to be a
value judgment, let it be free of racial or ethnic bias.[19]

Before turning to a brief but intense analysis of "social consciousness" among particular people, a general look at African
religion will be quite valuable. There are several cultures in
Africa (Black or Tropical Africa). The study of African religions is where anthropology and religion meet. It is necessary
to have a good understanding of various types of cultures
before attempting to understand the religion of a particular people. For example, there is the plain-hunting culture
of the Bushmen of the South and East. Then there are the
agrarian cultures, such as the *Congo culture* of West Africa,
with matriarchy (even women chiefs!) and reverence for ancestors and fertility cults, and the *palaeo-Nigritian culture* of the
Sudan and nearby territories, with patriarchy and reverence
for ancestral spirits at the center of its cult practice. These
are only representative. There are differences in physiology
among Africans. Africa has some of the smallest people in
the world (the Pygmies) as well as some of the tallest (the
Nilotic peoples). Even an expert linguist finds Africa a veri-
table forest. It follows that intense study of a religion among a

particular people with an interdisciplinary methodology is the only approach that will bear abundant fruit.

It is fortunate for the student of African religions that some basic beliefs and cult practices appear to be almost universal among black Africans. The absence of sacred texts is a distinct handicap for most Western philosophers and theologians, to say nothing of biblical exegetes. But this is somewhat overcome by a well-organized tribal or familial organization of society in which religion is closely associated with law and custom. The careful transmission of religious beliefs and practices through a cadre of prophets and priests has preserved the continuity of many African religions.

All African peoples seem to know of a supreme god, a "high god." He is Nyame, "the shining one" among the Ashanti. Among the Bantu of East Africa, he is Mulungu, "he above," and among the Pygmies he is Khmvum, "lord of animals." For the most part, the supreme god is associated with the sky or some other celestial phenomenon, such as the sun. He is far away, a *deus otiosus*. He is not the daily object of cult practice and is invoked mainly during emergencies. There are exceptions to this generalization, however. The supreme god Amman in the French Sudan enjoys regular worship at special altars and has his own priesthood.

Simply because of the inaccessibility of the high god, there emerged a great number of natural deities. Almost universally man has worshiped the forces of nature because his life and well-being are so tied to nature. Thus, nature as angry and feared is worshiped alongside nature as mother and friend. Thunder and pestilence are deified along with the earth and the sea. Because human life appears to be so close to animal life, animal worship and snake worship also are common.

The "culture hero" is important in many religious situations in Africa. He is the messenger of the high god and the founder and organizer of a tribe. He disappeared in a thunder storm and now lives in his altars and is incarnate in the chief or king. This culture bringer may be in human or animal shape. It is extremely interesting that Lanternari's study of postcolonial nativistic religious sects in Africa — Christian, Muslim, and traditional — indicates that the cultural hero tradition of African religious history is still a powerful force to reckon with.[20]

The reverence for ancestral spirits is a most important aspect of African religions. It is pan-African, but it is near universal among peoples with group families. This tradition receives less stress in West Africa because of a richly developed pantheon. Religious awe and devotion that cultivate the continuing fellowship and goodwill between the living and the "living dead" are at the heart of African religious belief and practice.

In describing the "primal worldview," John V. Taylor says:

> The sense of the personal totality of all being, and of a humanity which embraces the living, the dead and the divinities, fills the foreground in which this solidarity becomes sharply defined and directly experienced in the life of the extended family, the clan and the tribe. This is the context in which an African learns to say, I am because I participate. To him the individual is always an abstraction; Man is a family.[21]

The religious unit is usually the tribe. Outside the tribe and without contact with ancestral spirits, normal life is not considered possible. Everyone is admitted to the community through initiation. This initiation produces a very intense solidarity inside the "age class" — among one's own peer group.

Often inside the larger society there is a secret society with its own cult not known outside. In some cases this secret society includes all men who have gone through initiation. In other cases it constitutes a minor closed group among the men of the tribe to which the members are admitted after a special initiation. The society knows "the truth," acting as the guardian of justice and morals by punishing theft and adultery. Members of such a society often wear masks and costumes. The society is also a protector of property. Women and children are excluded. In some cases, however, women have parallel societies of their own.

These secret societies are socioreligious groups. The Poro society in Sierra Leone is an association of all male members of the tribe (the Mende tribe). The Poro society is controlled by spirits that men incarnate with their masks. These are the leaders who inherit their offices. At the initiation the inductees are said to be swallowed by the Poro spirit, and only when, during a period of isolation in the bush, they have been given instruction about the customs, songs, dances, spirits, and ethics of the tribe are they resurrected by divinity and reborn.

Another important example is the Komo society of the Bambara. Members of this society include all circumcised men. Its leader is a blacksmith who represents the culture-founding hero (ancestor). He is guardian of the altar and in charge of the inherited traditions of the society. Initiation takes place at night. Those initiated must swear not to reveal the secrets that will be imparted to them during the ceremony while drinking together from the blood of a sacrificed goat. Dances with masks are part of the ceremony, the Komo mask of the society being particularly terrifying. The society regulates life in the village and deals with the agrarian rites as well as with political decisions. This Komo society is the main pillar of the larger Bambara society.

The tribe is divided into a number of clans, each with its own totem. Members of the clan are not allowed to kill or eat their totem animal. The totem is not worshiped directly — it is regarded as representing the mythical ancestor who was such an animal. Community life is thoroughly organized. There is the tribe, the clan, the patrilineal kin group within the clan, the family, the bilineal kindred, the mother's brothers and their families, the sister's family, the field-working party, the age class, and age groups.

As one moves from piety to ethics, one discovers that African religions have secular goals. What matters is to ensure a livelihood and to satisfy needs as well as to find protection against dangers and evil powers, especially those from the spirit world.

Moral commands are communicated at initiation, thus having religious sanction. Someone has pointed out that the Mende tribe of Sierra Leone finds its ethics in the last seven Commandments. Most African peoples have similar moral codes, but one must allow for variety among differing environments. Respect for parents and solidarity within the group are particularly highly valued. Infringement of the moral law is believed to lead to divine punishment. Illness is often regarded as punishment for sin, but malevolent spirits and the magic of sorcerers also may cause illness.[22]

This essay is intended as a prolegomenon to interdisciplinary investigation into African religions. I am suggesting a subjective-objective approach by the Western investigator. While the auto-ethnographic approach of Christian Gaba is necessary, it will be incomplete, however profound, because of the subjectivism inherent in studying one's own people and ancestral faith. The scholar should not, on the other hand, be indifferent and unappreciative of religious phenomena. Religion should be a "live option" in the experience of the participant-observer. Religion is not to be studied from the inside or outside alone. It is often understood best by a combination approach. Those who have a faith, who are not merely studying religions or "experimenting" with them out of sheer necessity, are able to assess what another's religion means to him. In this way, they empathetically move inside another's faith; but because they stand outside, they are able to discover weaknesses in another's tradition, not because they consider their own faith superior but because they are aware of the meaning of vital religion. This is the reason that religion at its best is prophetic as well as priestly, and rational as well as volitional and emotional.

Applying this general outlook to certain "social and ethical" concerns, we have discovered that African religions embrace the total life of the individual and the community. God consciousness and social consciousness are one. To belong to a community is to accept the divinity that gives sanction to the laws and customs undergirding the life and activities of the group. Our main concern here has been historical. We have been concerned primarily with what religion has meant to Africans. What religion may mean to them in the face of urbanization and secularization belongs to another time and another task.

Chapter 9

Africanisms and
Spiritual Strivings

A great difficulty faced by blacks is that of justifying Christianity as practiced by whites. Blacks are now facing what some appropriately refer to as a "Second Reconstruction."[1] Blacks face a "turning the clock back" approach to racial justice. Neglect — benign and malicious — is descriptive of the new mood. Repression in law enforcement and legal conservatism are likewise having an open season. After a decade of rapid strides through the courts, legislation, business and labor institutions, and religious and social bodies, we have presently in vogue a well-planned slowdown in efforts for racial justice. The belief that suppression is the solution to all human ills is flirting with disaster. It is within such a context that blacks must chart their religious affirmations.

Carter G. Woodson is correct in pointing to the fact that the religion of most blacks in this country, and to a great extent in Africa, is the oppressor's interpretation of Christianity.[2] It is obvious why the black man becomes indignant and fearlessly attacks Christianity on the grounds of being sham and hypocrisy. The argument that Christianity is all right, although the oppressor may not be living up to it, does not satisfy the critics. The reason is rather obvious. The black man has no other interpretation than that which he has received from the American or European. The situation has therefore become

Originally published in *Journal of Religious Thought* 30 (spring–summer 1973): 16–27.

more critical as the days have gone by, and the future of the Christian faith is uncertain among blacks.

All people need a temporal as well as a spatial home. All people need some appreciation of their past as an index to their present. I have traveled with white friends who have pointed proudly to certain monuments and buildings that remind them of their past. It is exciting to be with someone who is reliving and reenacting his or her past — who through certain signposts is able to bring the past to the present. I was with a New Englander recently who from memory was able to retell the history of the colony of Connecticut mainly through his own blood relatives. I was not able, however, to associate my past with his. His past was glorious. My ancestors came to this country in chains, and we still are not free.

The black man's ethnic past is different, even if we move in the same social, economic, and intellectual circles as whites. Our "historical identification" is different from our "participation identification." Though we are in the same socioeconomic class with whites, our ethclass (the intersection of ethnicity and social class) is different from that of whites; our peoplehood as blacks has a different locus.[3]

In a conference on black religious experience held at Howard University during February 1970, Professor Charles Long of the Divinity School of the University of Chicago made the point that blacks as well as Jews need a home. Throughout the centuries Jews in many lands have looked homeward. Many generations of Jews lived and died without a real home but have had a symbolic home. Likewise, according to Long, when blacks speak of Africa, they refer to their ancestral home in the same manner in which pre-Zionist Jews looked to Israel. Some African leaders, no less than would-be colonizers, blacks and whites, have misunderstood the meaning of "symbolic Africa." "Literal Africa" is a myth to most American blacks. In spite of all attempts to sponsor "back to Africa" movements, whether by white segregationists or black separatists, few blacks have responded.[4] What the black man needs in Africa is not a real but a symbolic home. Having been brought to the New World, most blacks consider this as their real home. Their past, however, must be explored if they are to contribute to a multiracial culture.

Again, the invisible or oral history of blacks is to be distinguished from the ideological history of whites. J. A. Tillinghast, in his book *The Negro in Africa and America,* promises to provide an understanding of the Negro character against his African past.[5] He concludes that Africa is a land of great barbarity — almost beyond description — and that the Negro is naturally inadequately endowed for full citizenship. The work is well documented by scholars — mostly French and English colonizers. Tillinghast, a Southerner who studied at a northern university, gives a frank point of view that is held openly in the South and latently in the North — the myth of the inherent inferiority of the Negro. To this end, great emphasis is placed on the "heathen religious practices" and "gross immorality" of Africans. A black man looking at the behavior of white slave traders could return the compliment.

The history of the church and theology has been against the dignity of the black man. Not only has history, as written and interpreted, omitted the black man's positive contribution, but it has been interpreted so as to sponsor the myth of black inferiority. Thus, history, religious and secular, has provided a false image of the black man to such an extent that he is not able to be respected or to respect himself. This is the intended result of white ideological history. According to Charles Long, Americans suffer from a superiority complex vis-à-vis Africa and Asia and from an inferiority complex vis-à-vis Europe.[6] It is my candid observation that white Americans read history "backwards." Being convinced of the inferiority of blacks in their midst, they associate this assumption with their African ancestry. Inferiority is more rigorously applied to blacks in Central and South America and to Africans than it is to Asians generally.

The history of our Afro-American past is capable of a positive treatment. The roots of a black theology are found in the history of black religious experience. Black religion definitely appears to have traces of African influence. Evidence for this is now observable in Brazil, Central America, the Deep South (i.e., South Carolina and New Orleans), and in mass denominations and religious sects and cults in the dark ghettos of the North and urban South (i.e., among Baptist and Pentecostal groups). Thus, there is empirical or phenomenological data to substantiate the persistence of "Africanisms" in black religious experience — at least from West Africa to the Americas. Evidence from other parts of Africa, save the Interior — some 1,800 miles east of the West Coast, is less easy to establish. Most historians and cultural anthropologists prefer to take a firm stand in West Africa and trace the influence from there.

Because of tribal, familial, and religious differences among Africans — generalizations should be avoided when possible. Our main concern is with traditional or more spontaneous religious experience, even though Islamic and Christian influences were undoubtedly present among Africans who were deported as slaves to the New World. A pattern of transmission of these religious traditions is observable in stages that may be somewhat dated — though not precisely so.

There was the period of "inception," or the "primitive" religious period. This period reflected animism, fetishism, and voodooism. A careful study of this period requires some appreciation for this type of religious expression that is found throughout the world — among early European and Asiatic peoples as much as among Africans. Phenomenology of religion, history of religion, history, psychology, sociology, archeology, cultural anthropology, and ethnomusicology are some of the areas of investigation helpful in this interpretative task. We insist that a rich religious heritage has been preserved in spite of all repressions. The fact that slaves were treated as property and considered as heathen was a boon to this cultural carryover. Religion, as they knew it, enabled the slaves

to endure the ordeal of the Middle Passage and the brutality
of their enslavement.

E. Franklin Frazier is correct in pointing to the shattering effects resulting from uprooting and transporting blacks.
According to Frazier, this destroyed their traditional culture
and broke up their social organization. It destroyed the worldview that had held their lives together and had provided
meaning for their existence. Africans had a developed system
of religious beliefs as well as a well-defined social orientation.
In the crisis of slavery, Africans appealed to their ancestors
and their gods. Some took their own lives, believing that in
so doing they would return to their homeland. Others submit-
ted to their fate and sought a meaning for their existence in
the new white man's world. Those slaves most isolated from
whites engaged in religious practices that were undoubtedly
based on African survivals. According to Frazier, in the course
of time, whites brought slaves increasingly under the influence
of the Christian religion. Memories of African gods were lost
or forgotten. This deculturation was effected by efforts on the
part of whites to prevent any resurgence of African religion.[7]
Frazier insists that even the "shout songs" and "holy dances"
of black Sea Islanders of South Carolina and Georgia were
addressed to the white man's God and were more influenced
by Christian ideology than by the African background. The
black man therefore adapted Christianity to his experience in
the New World. The spirituals and the "invisible church" were
the results.[8]

Frazier's position is one of almost total deculturation of the
black man from his African past. It follows that there were
no significant religious survivals. The black man's acceptance
of Christianity was emotional, pietistic and escapist. LeRoi
Jones, in his essay "Afro-Christian Music and Religion," sees
evidence of a definite survival of African influence in black
religion.[9] Even when the black man was forbidden by his
captors to worship in the old ways, his immediate reaction

was to worship in secret. Jones says: "Many of the 'superstitions' of the Negroes that the Whites thought 'charming' were holdovers from African religions. Even today in many Southern rural areas, strange mixtures of voodoo, or other primarily African fetish religions, and Christianity exist."[10]

Africans came from an intensely religious culture, where religion was a daily concern and not a one-hour-per-week reaffirmation. Africans could not function as human beings without religion. Christians exploited this built-in propensity toward religion among African slaves. Slaveholders proclaimed Christianity in such a way as to enable blacks to be spiritually free while physically shackled in chains. They counseled obedience and the acceptance of enslavement in this life while looking forward to heavenly bliss.[11] Jones says:

> The slave masters also learned early that the Africans who had begun to accept the Christian ethic or even some crude part of its dogma, were less likely to run away or start rebellions or uprisings. Christianity, as it was first given to the slaves...was to be used strictly as a code of conduct which would enable its devotees to participate in an afterlife; it was from its very inception among the black slaves, a slave ethic. It acted as a great pacifier and palliative, although it also produced a great inner strength among the devout and an almost inhuman indifference to pain.[12]

The white man's intentions were for Christianity to make the slave happy with his new lot. In some sense the acceptance of Christianity was the beginning of the perception of Africa as a foreign place. Christianity was a type of metaphysical resolution for the slave's natural yearnings for freedom — it literally made life easier for him. The black man's desire to cross Jordan and "see his Lord" meant that he no longer wished to return to Africa. Jones observes, "It took the slave's mind off Africa, or material freedom, and proposed that if the black man wished to escape the filthy paternalism and cruelty of slavery, he wait, at least until death, when he could be transported peacefully and majestically to the Promised Land."[13]

But the African has an oriental mind, and even without learning, he appeared to understand the message of the Bible better than his white teachers. The tragic aftermath is that whites believed their own false version of the Bible. Blacks loved the Bible because it speaks of God's concern for an oppressed people. The struggles of the Jews and their promised land was a strong analogy for the slaves.

> Mary, don't you weep an' Marthie don't you moan,
> Mary, don't you weep an' Marthie don't you moan,
> Pharaoh's army got drown-ded,
> Oh, Mary, don't you weep.[14]

The religious imagery of the Negro's Christianity is full of references to the suffering and hopes of the oppressed Jews of biblical times. Consequently, entrance into heaven and release from earthly bondage were united in the mind of slaves. Prechurch "praise houses" became the social focal points of Negro life.[15]

The period of "inception" was followed by a period of acculturation, religious as well as cultural. John Hope Franklin points out that notwithstanding the heterogeneity in African life, there were sufficient common experiences for Negroes in the New World to cooperate in establishing new customs and traditions that reflected their African background. According to Franklin, two acculturative processes were taking place. On the one hand, there was the interaction of the various African cultures that produced a different set of customs and practices rooted deep in African experiences. At the same time, there was an interaction of African and Western cultures that changed the culture patterns of both groups. For instance, where European patterns were weak, African survivals were strongest. Franklin concludes that in

Brazil and the Caribbean Islands, due to successful revolts, transplantation of an African way of life was made possible to a considerable degree. Elsewhere one can observe the process taking place in a gradual way, but some African culture is an obvious fact. In religion, Franklin observes that there are divinations and various cult practices with an African background.[16]

The African, according to Franklin, came out of an experience that was sufficiently entrenched to make possible the persistence of some customs and traditions. In the conflict of cultures, those practices survive whose values and superiority give them the strength and tenacity to do so. Franklin concludes:

> African survivals in America also suggest a pronounced resiliency of African institutions. There had been sufficient intertribal and interstate intercourse to give Africans the important experience of adopting many of the practices of those with whom they came into contact, while at the same time retaining much of their earlier way of life. After all, perhaps the survival of Africanisms in the New World was as great as it was because of the refusal of the members of the dominant group in America to extend, without reservations, their own culture to the Negroes whom they brought over.[17]

Ruby F. Johnson refers to the second phase of Negro religious adjustment as the "developmental" stage.[18] The developmental stage was one during which religion acquired a more meaningful, practical form as the Negro visualized the essence of the Christian doctrine and applied it in a manner that best served his needs.[19] This phase of Negro religion begins with the Emancipation Proclamation and extends to World War I (1863–1914). Heavenly elements were diminished, and there was greater emphasis on securing civil and social rights supported by active participation in government and social life.[20]

There is some question in mind about the extremely active role of religion during this period. Blacks did read the Bible and have their own churches, and the black church was a viable social and political institution. But it was a period given to compromises, and black religious Uncle Toms were numerous and quite useful to whites during this time. Protest was vigorous and relentless on the part of antebellum blacks between 1800 and 1860. Black preachers, schooled and unlearned alike, were the great incendiaries of that period. Not only Nat Turner, the prophet of revenge and revolt, but numerous black ministers were the helpful supporters of Frederick Douglass and other abolitionists. Perhaps religious "protesters" were the rule during the antebellum period and "Uncle Toms" the rule during the immediate post–Civil War period; but in both instances, exceptions alter the rule. With this word of caution, we can consider the significance of the so-called developmental stage.

When the black man arrived, he "remembered his past" and expected to return to Africa. Once it became apparent that he must adjust to a new and permanent situation, a new stage of religion emerged. Here the insights of Viktor Frankl's logotherapy have been suggestive to me. Frankl, a Jewish psychiatrist incarcerated in the German death camps during World War II, tells of the various stages of consciousness through which the prisoners passed. He describes the first stage as shock — that is, the prisoners could not believe that what was happening was *really* happening to them. It was a "delusion of reprieve" — somewhat like that experienced by a condemned man just before his execution. Under such circumstances, one often gets the illusion that he might be reprieved at the very last moment.[21] Lerone Bennett has compared the torture of the Middle Passage endured by black slaves with the inhumanity of Auschwitz.

After the delusion of reprieve, according to Frankl, comes apathy — "a kind of emotional death." After being consumed by longing, one is seized by disgust. Frankl says:

Apathy, the blunting of the emotions and the feeling that one could not care any more, were the symptoms arising during the second stage of the prisoner's psychological reactions, and which eventually made him insensitive to daily and hourly beatings. By means of this insensitivity, the prisoner soon surrounded himself with a very necessary protective shell.[22]

Frankl goes on to say that mental agony caused by injustice hurts more than physical pain.[23] The most painful part of beatings is the insult they imply. Parenthetically, as one studies the narratives of black slaves, this appears to be an apt description of the tragic experience of that inhuman institution.[24] Frankl observes that in spite of an almost complete "cultural hibernation" in the death camps, politics and religion were exceptions. He writes concerning religion:

The religious interest of the prisoners, as far and as soon as it developed, was the most sincere imaginable. The depth and vigor of religious belief often surprised and moved a new arrival. Most impressive in this connection were improvised prayers or services in the corner of a hut, or in the darkness of the locked cattle truck in which we were brought back from a distant work site, tired, hungry and frozen in our ragged clothing.[25]

Frankl continues:

In spite of all the enforced physical and mental primitiveness of the life in a concentration camp, it was possible for spiritual life to deepen. Sensitive people who were used to rich intellectual life may have suffered much pain . . . but the damage to their inner selves was less. They were able to retreat from their terrible surroundings to a life of inner riches and spiritual freedom. Only in this way can one explain the apparent paradox that some prisoners of a less hardy makeup often seemed to survive camp life better than did those of a robust nature.[26]

Between slavery and the death camps, one may point to an analogy in human tragedy. But in both cases faith and survival were wed. In both cases innocent humans were victimized by savage fellowmen and stripped to "naked existence." They were confronted by the threat of nonbeing. Only a firm religious hold on life could carry one across such an abyss. Frankl's psychoanalytic description of his experiences in the death camps, together with a search for meaning, casts some light on the psychology of black religious experience in its various phases.

What happened to our black fathers and mothers during those dark days in some ways happened to us. Their religious expression represents our "spiritual strivings." Our religious heritage is one that has been purified through the fires of suffering. A deep appreciation of the meaning and agency of religion through that period is precious to us.

> Stony the road we trod,
> Bitter the chast'ning rod,
> Felt in the days when hope unborn had died;
> Yet with a steady beat,
> Have not our weary feet
> Come to the place for which our fathers sighed?
> We have come over a way that with tears has been
>   watered,
> We have come, treading our path through the blood of
>   the slaughtered,
> Out from the gloomy past,
> Till now we stand at last
> Where the white gleam of our bright star is cast.[27]

Once the black man became aware that he was here to stay, he had to find the means of survival in a cruel and heartless world. Religion — primitive and Christian — served as a great preservative for the black man through the years. Religion comforted and strengthened him. It provided an antidote for loneliness. It gave him superhuman powers of courage and endurance and enabled him to find meaning and fulfillment for life not merely in spite of the injustice and suffering endured but in some sense because of it. The black man, like Frankl, but without the knowledge of Freud, Jung, or Adler, used his suffering to find spiritual fulfillment. Instead of giving in to insanity or giving up through suicide, black men under these inhuman conditions dared to hope for a better day.

A third and final stage of black religion in the American situation is the "transitional" stage. Ruby Johnson describes this stage as one that retains some of the emotional elements of the more traditional phases. This is true because all religions are emotive but also because religion serves as a social outlet for blacks. The decline of emotionalism represents a crisis for some who formerly relied on the cathartic results of such religious expression. At the same time, during this transitional stage there is a transference of religion to this world. Religion, in this case Afro-American Christianity, becomes politically alert, socially active, and intellectually reflective.[28]

I will equate this phase of black religion generally with the period from 1914 through 1966 to the emergence of black power. The emphasis on race relations during this period is reflected in black religious expression. From Du Bois to King, the emphasis is on one-way integration. The undergirding assumption is that "white is beautiful" and that black Christians should join white churches. Perhaps for the first time since being in the New World, the black man was in danger of forsaking almost completely his Afro-American religious heritage for an opportunity to be admitted to membership in white churches. Joseph Washington, in *Black Religion*, while ridiculing black folk religion as a sentimental Jesusology, sees ultimate salvation in white Christian bodies.[29] Washington says: "Religion for the Negro is inherited and changed by the contemporary mood without reference to the theological dimension of faith. His religious institutions exist without any meaningful goals, with the sole exception of providing refuge for the disinherited."[30]

Washington believed that Negroes wanted integration —
that is, they were willing to accept white cultural values. Since
Negro congregations exist essentially because of social ties,
they now have the responsibility of going out of business.
Washington concluded, "It is incumbent upon the Negro now
to close his house of worship and enter the white congregations of his choice en masse."[31]

It would be woefully dishonest of me to say that Washington still holds this view. From this pro-white position, he
moved to a pro-black position in *Politics of God,* in which
he speaks of black Christians as the "chosen people." In his
most recent work, *Black and White Power Subreption,* he has
escalated his militancy to such an extent that he is not merely
anti-white but now sees guerrilla warfare as perhaps the only
answer to the racial crisis.

Without pursuing Washington further, we can see that he
has passed through a rapid transition of his own. In some
ways he is a bridge between the integrationist approach to
race relations and the implications of black power. His lack
of appreciation for the black religious heritage at the outset
makes it difficult for him to make significant use of black
religion in a constructive restatement of the Christian faith.
The black man's understanding of the Christian faith is Afro-
American. Between him and Africa stands more than 350
years of history. His culture and worldview has been transformed by the Judeo-Christian and Greco-Roman cultural
complex. "Africanisms" and "spiritual strivings" remain, but
they exist in a Euro-American context. The faith that has sustained us is with us still, but it now needs to be articulated
against its past with a bold consciousness of our needs and
aspirations as a people in the present and in the future.

> God of our weary years,
> God of our silent tears,
> Thou who hast brought us
> Thus far on the way;

Thou who hast by Thy might
Led us into the light,
Keep us forever in the path, we pray.
Lest our feet stray from the places,
Our God, where we met Thee.
Lest our hearts, drunk with
The wine of the world, we forget Thee;
Shadowed beneath Thy hand
May we forever stand,
True to our God,
True to our native land.[32]

Chapter 10

Traditional African Religion and Christian Theology

Introduction to the Problem

Much has been written recently on the contextualization of theology in Africa by African theologians. A fruitful dialogue has been initiated between Afro-American and African theologians. African theologians have participated in discussions among third world theologians. My task in writing is somewhat distinct from all these efforts. It is, however, related to most of these discussions. As an Afro-American and as a theologian trained and functioning in the West, I have assumed the task of looking at traditional African religion and lifting out elements that might contribute to Christian theology.

I am dealing with "traditional" African religion. I use "religion" here rather than "religions" because I am concerned with the common characteristics of religious experience in this body of religious experience that may prove useful in Christian theological discourse.

Dialogue with a Living Tradition

The historical study of African religion is necessary if we are to understand contemporary developments. Our dialogue is to

Originally published in *Studia Africana* 1 (fall 1979): 206–18. This essay is the result of a lecture given 27 May 1978, during the Conference on Contemporary African Religions at Unification of Theological Seminary, Barrytown, New York.

take place with a living tradition, a dynamic religion in which there are new areas of application as well as continuities with the past.

African traditional religion was never wholly particularist. Religious concepts, symbols, and practices had a currency wider than other elements of an ethnically based culture. Religious movements, cults, and objects were subject to historical diffusion. On the other hand, African traditional religion had an ethnic basis in the sense that it was articulated through the sociopolitical institutions of the tribe. However much religious concepts and symbols transcended the horizons of tribal culture, the African could experience his religion and give expression to it only through the structures of the tribe.

Multiple adaptations to differing environments in relative isolation produced the fragmented, autonomous groupings that we call tribes. It was in the tribe that African traditional religion received its visible expression. Authority was basically politico-religious, and professional priesthoods and other cultic offices or forms of religious dedication represented partial approaches or specializations within the religious systems taken as a whole. At the territorial level the hierarchy of family heads, clan leaders, elders, or chiefs presided over religious rituals, led the people in worship, and took the initiative in creating and manipulating religious institutions such as oracles or rites of initiation.

Tribe loyalty is still important, but it has undergone a radical transformation. From being a more or less autonomous political unit, it has now developed into an ideology of unity or a symbol of cultural identity. African traditional religion coexists with the missionary religions: Christianity, Judaism, and Islam. In addition, new, visible forms of African traditional religion are coming into existence — for example, "communities of affliction." These are voluntary associations, more or less religious in character, that cater to sick people and people in need of status definition. They usually include a form of spirit mediumship and attach much importance to glossolalia. These movements have affinity with Pentecostalism and faith healing.

African religious traditions also find a new lease on life in the independent churches. These are listed as belonging to three main categories: Christian, Hebraist, and neo-traditional. In the Christian type the differences with the parent mission churches are historical rather than theological. In the Hebraist type there is found a form of neo-Judaism with varying emphasis on aspects of the Old Testament tradition. In the neo-traditional type there is a conscious revival or development of African traditional religion. It is in the neo-traditional type that the most distinctive African religious roots are found. Finally, there is the presence of African traditional religious experience in the historic churches and in Islam.[1]

Ways of Thinking of African Peoples

African Protestant writers have been quicker than Catholic writers to interest themselves in traditional African religious beliefs. The reason seems to be that Roman Catholics need a philosophical foundation for theology. Protestants, on the other hand, can develop a theology based "on the Biblical faith of Africans, which speaks to the African soul."[2] This implies using African categories of thought arising out of the experience of African peoples.

This does not imply that African Protestant theologians are not cautious regarding what they use from traditional religion. John Mbiti acknowledges that he is not fully certain how much he can use from African traditional religion. He asks, "How far can, or should we, regard African religiosity as a *praeparatio evangelica?*"[3] He concludes that he is sure that this background cannot be ignored. E. Bolaji Idowu asserts that we should apprehend African spiritual values with the African mind while possessing the requisite knowledge of the fundamental facts of the faith that are to be expressed and disseminated in an indigenous idiom.[4]

With their neo-scholastic training, Catholics assumed that there could be no African theology without a prior discovery of an African philosophy; this search has been a disappointment, mainly because of a limited view of philosophy. Protestants, on the other hand, have been less restrictive in their attitude toward philosophy and have refused to be restricted by it. Mbiti asserts that behind the religious diversity in traditional Africa, there is a single philosophy. He admits that the interpretation of African life through word and action may involve subjective judgment. An African neo-scholastic would not be satisfied with a subjective approach to philosophizing. Such a thinker would want to build a rational, conceptual system out of African traditional thought comparable to Western philosophy.

Alexis Kagame, an African neo-scholastic, illustrates this viewpoint. He admits that the question of an African philosophy has arisen because of the encounter with European philosophy. It is through the inspiration from European philosophy that the African thinks of trying to express the traditional thought of his people as a conceptual system. Kagame accepts Aristotle as his guide because he believes that Aristotle has a universal breadth and relevance.

At one point Africans were flattered that Europeans had taken their original ideas seriously enough to build a rational, conceptual system out of them. They saw this as a corrective to the attitude of Levy-Bruhl[5] and Emil Ludwig, who asserted the incapacity of Africans to think conceptually. Edwin Smith reports that in a conversation with Emil Ludwig, he explained that missionaries were teaching Africans about God. Ludwig was perplexed and responded: "How can the untutored African conceive God?...Deity is a philosophical concept which savages are incapable of framing."[6]

It is understood, then, why the work of Placide Tempels on Bantu philosophy generated considerable excitement.

With Aristotle and Aquinas as guides, Tempels and his pupil Alexis Kagame explored the abstract ideas of some Bantu languages. They discussed African parallels of concepts such as being, existence, and causality. They developed an ontological-epistemological structure on the Bantu understanding of "vital force." In this way, they revealed fresh and typically African emphases and categories. But these philosophical constructs were based almost exclusively on linguistic analyses, language structure, and the range of meaning of particular words. The main literary source was the corpus of proverbs, assumed to contain the wisdom of the African and the names and attributes of the supreme being. In fact, proverbs are often cynical statements about life that may rest upon observation and experience only, while the etymology of names, minus other kinds of evidence, can encourage all kinds of suppositions and fantasies.[7]

A part of the problem is a disdain by philosophers of symbolic thought. Symbolic ways of thinking were not considered to meet acceptable standards as far as the cogency of reasoning is concerned. It was felt that symbols could not be studied systematically as symbols. It was held that they had to be transformed into reasoned concepts and that every people had to evolve in their thinking from a symbolic state into a philosophical or scientific state. The work of Claude Levi-Strauss and the use of his methods on African materials established the fact that structural analysis of symbols is possible. Furthermore, it was asserted that one could remain within the scope of rational thought without doing away with concrete symbols and at the same time articulate and render them more intelligible.

The interpretation of symbols is not limited to verbal symbols. Symbolic action is perhaps more important. Victor Turner's studies have complemented the work of Levi-Strauss at this point. African ritual, according to Turner, is a configuration of manufactured symbols with varied structures and different levels of meaning. Turner's concept of the "positional meaning" of symbols, according to which they are linked to other related contexts in the whole range of culture, is a way of relating parts to the whole. Okot p'Bitek has indicated in this perspective that the task of those who study African religion and philosophy is to photograph as many details as possible of the way of life of the people. After this is accomplished, then one should point out the connections among and relevances of the different parts and their ultimate relation to the whole of life.[8]

Mbiti provides one creative attempt at African religious thinking. He asserts that linear time moving from creation to consummation is foreign to African thinking. There is a past and a present but a virtual absence of the future. Time is made up of events. The future has no independent existence, since events that compose time have not occurred in it. The future is therefore either *potential time* or *no time*. Africans must experience time for it to make sense. Time moves backwards rather than forwards. These two dimensions, past and present, are the dominant periods in the life of the individual and the community.

Two Swahili terms, *Zamani* and *Sasa*, designate these two periods of time, past and present. The two time periods are said to overlap — there is no necessary separation between them. *Sasa* is not just the "now of time." It is the period in which people exist and in which they project themselves primarily into the past and to a lesser extent into the future. *Sasa* is "micro-time." What is future is almost actualized and nearly passed away. So vague is the future as anticipation that East African languages do not provide a word for the future in their vocabulary, Mbiti observes.

The *Zamani* period is "macro-time." It is past, present, and whatever future there is. It overlaps with *Sasa*. Before events are absorbed into *Zamani,* they must first occur in *Sasa*. Then they move backward into *Zamani,* in which everything finds its termination. According to Mbiti, *Zamani* is the storehouse for all phenomena and events, a vast ocean of time in which everything gets absorbed into reality. *Sasa* and *Zamani* have both quantity and quality (e.g., good, long, short, bad, etc.) in relation to a particular phenomenon.

Chronology is reckoned in traditional society by "phenomenon calendars" rather than numerical calendars. Time is not measured for its own sake but according to important happenings. Lunar months have names in relation to harvest events and other activities such as hunting. A year is complete when the seasons and activities of a complete year have been realized. Africans expect the years to come and go in an endless rhythm like that of day and night and the waxing and waning of the moon.[9]

Mbiti helps us to appreciate the place of myth in African traditional thought. History flows backward. There is no future golden age, no belief in progress, and no end time. The center of gravity in African thought is *Zamani*. Therefore, African thought is preoccupied with myths in creation. There are many myths explaining creation, the first man, the fall of man, the coming of death. What we observe is a history of origins that lays the foundation for the nation's existence. There are no myths of the *Endzeit,* but myths of the *Urzeit* are abundant. Humans look back from whence they came and are certain that nothing shall bring this world to a conclusion. Mbiti writes: "Human life follows a rhythm of nature which nothing can destroy: birth, puberty, initiation, marriage, procreation, old age, death, entry into the company of the departed and eventually into the company of spirits. Another rhythm is also at work: that of days and nights, months (moons), seasons and years. . . . This twofold rhythm of Nature is everlasting."[10]

It will be necessary to return to Mbiti again, but for the present we wish to explore briefly the role of myth in African traditional religion and philosophy. We are not concerned with the content of African mythology but with myth as a way of thinking. Charles Long, a black historian of religion, provides some helpful perspectives on mythical thinking. Long rightly points out that we affirm a rationalistic form of thinking and that we usually consign "myth" to the fanciful imagination of the human mind. We therefore consider peoples and cultures given to mythical thinking as unreal. Some theologians, Long recalls, abhor the use of myth because they think it refers to the fanciful and unreal.

Long asserts that the study of peoples who live in myth-making cultures would be a corrective to this misinformed attitude. Myth, according to Long, is a true story — a story about reality. It is impossible to understand the reality and being of peoples from myth-making cultures unless one understands their reality in relationship to myth.[11] Long writes: "When we speak of understanding their reality, we are speaking of their reality in the precise sense of their human presence, their specificity and qualitative meaning in time and space. We are not denying the possibility of understanding them on other levels, e.g., as biological beings, but such an understanding tells us little, if anything, about their humanness."[12]

Myths are not true in the literal sense, according to Long. But literariness is not to be equated with truth. Mythical thinking is not to be identified with logic. On the other hand, it is not illogical or prelogical. Myth is at the same time logical and illogical, logical and magical, rational and irrational. It represents a man's initial confrontation with the power in life. The beings referred to in myth are forms of power grasped existentially. In myth, expression is given to man's reaction to life as a source of power and being. The word and content of myth are revelations of power.[13]

The veneration of the earth, totemic animals, and ancestors in myth-making cultures make it clear that the apprehension of life as potency is remembered, according to Long, that the coming of the rational does not mean the end to the mythic. The mythic and the rational coexist. The mythic apprehension of reality is not destroyed in the evolutionary process.

Alongside of the rational mythic remains a mode through which we have access to the real.

There are human experiences on the personal and cultural levels that can be expressed only in symbolic forms. These meanings are in many cases the most profound meanings in our lives because they symbolize the specificity of our human situation. Myth is a symbolic ordering that makes clear how the world is present for man.[14] In religious thought the use of analogy may be an attempt to deal discursively with symbolic forms of human expression. Depth psychology has made it clear that the most profound relationships of human existence cannot be rendered adequately on the level of conscious and rational thought. Long writes, "The most profound symbols of human reality seem to include as a necessary ingredient a dimension of reality which is more than human and more than natural."[15]

Long tells us that the cosmogonic myths, the myths of creation, convey profound meanings. The creation myth is an expression of man's cosmic orientation. This involves one's apprehension of time and space, one's participation in the natural order, the relationships between humans, and the ultimate powers that sustain human existence in the world.[16]

In this section we have looked briefly at method in African thought. We have concluded that there are both similarities and differences between African and Western ways of thinking. It is obvious to me that Africans have much in common with Asians as distinguished from Western modes of thought. Thus far few African scholars have done serious work in either the history of religion or comparative religion. This makes the work of black scholars such as Charles Long doubly important. We need to know that literalness and logic do not necessarily equal truth, that mythic and/or symbolic ways of thinking are up to date and that they touch life at a profound level of meaning. This understanding would unlock for us the context in much of African traditional religious experience is expressed.

The Content of Africa's Contribution to Christian Theology

Before I read the works by African religious scholars, I had concluded that the subject of African traditional religion was unmanageable. It appeared that the diversity of tribal customs, religious systems, languages, and many other factors were too vast for any Westerner to tackle. This appeared to be the case, notwithstanding the fact that my study of non-Western religions had been extensive. Through reading Mbiti and especially Idowu, the subject matter became more within the range of my vision. I discovered that African religion, at the core, is similar across Black Africa. The beliefs in a supreme god, lesser spirits, and reverence for ancestors are held in common. These are the *esse,* the vital core beliefs of African traditional religion. Furthermore, I discovered that the ethno-theologians interpreted these basic beliefs in such a manner as to relate to biblical faith. Studying African religion at the same time as I was discovering the black religious heritage was a reinforcement experience, for in some ways we are dealing with one continuous religious tradition. Of course, there is much discontinuity as well, but the continuity makes the excursion into African religion more easily understood.[17]

According to Osadolor Imasogie, monotheism is the only adequate descriptive term for African traditional religion. There are lesser spirits or divinities, but these are regarded as having been created and appointed ministers by the supreme being. However, the place given these divinities is so conspicuous that monotheism must be qualified in such a way that this prominence is maintained while the underlying monotheistic motif is not obscured. Imasogie elects to use "bureaucratic monotheism" to describe African traditional religion. He sees this as appropriate because of the relationship between divinities and sociopolitical patterns of African society. African society is highly organized — it is hierarchical in nature. Kings are at the top. Kings appointed ministers to see to the day-to-day activities of their subjects. Various African languages have specific names for the supreme being as opposed to generic names for the divinities. The divinities are mainly derived from the personification of various aspects of nature that symbolize the providence of the supreme being.[18]

God in traditional African religion is a creator and provident god. God to Africans was never a *deus otiosus* — a deistic god. The names and attributes of God reflect an understanding of God as good, merciful, just, and caring. God is a father or mother. Africans often say, "God has been merciful," or "He has been good to me." God can overrule the power of the ancestors and spirits. Africans often display a childlike faith toward God. Peter Bolink writes: "For most traditional believers God is a *Deus Remotus,* which is something different from a *Deus Otiosus,* a functionless God. Though He is often felt to be unapproachable... He is believed to be at work in and behind all that happens and exists."[19]

Bolink also observes, "European Christians who find it extremely difficult to relate Sunday's worship to Monday's work, could learn from African believers to recapture a consistent religious experience of life and this would be a real spiritual enrichment to them."[20]

Mbiti, in his study of the names of God, unearths several important attributes of God held by traditional believers. Two of these are God's active involvement and creative involvement. The names of God speak about the work or activities of God. Africans conceive of God as an active Being, as personal, and as one who manifests himself through what he does. He observes that Africans are not given to much meditation in religious matters; instead, they celebrate their religious life. God is therefore sought in action rather than in pure contemplation. God is likewise related to the created universe. God's presence and power are manifest in and through natural objects and phenomena. God is intimately associated with the universe as its creator and sustainer, but the universe itself is a manifestation of God.[21] Mbiti is struck by the similarities between the traditional names for God and those used in the Bible.[22]

Aylward Shorter pulls together the "content" of Africa's contribution to religion. He speaks of the following: (1) a sense of religious wholeness; (2) symbolism as a means of communication; (3) fecundity — physical generation, life, and the sharing of life; (4) man-community; and (5) the relationship between human and spiritual beings — for example, ancestor reverence, the relation between the living and the dead.[23]

Africans affirm wholeness of thought as well as wholeness of life. Religious experience permeates the whole person and all relationships for life and even beyond death. Basil S. Matthews lifts up this truth-finding attribute of Africans that is executed conjointly by body, mind, and spirit. Matthews points to Leopold Sédar Senghor, the poet and philosopher of Négritude, as a fitting example.[24] Senghor describes mythology (e.g., imagery) as "the symbolic articulation of objective truth...the incarnation of ideas."[25] Senghor observes that it is through symbolic structures and operations of music, dance, literature, rhythms, and colors that Africans assimilate themselves with "the Other" and that this is the best pathway to knowledge.[26]

The use of this concept of Négritude by French-speaking Africans is a good meeting point between Africans and all people of African descent. The quest for an "African personality" began in Paris with an encounter between Afro-American persons of letters and such people as Aimé Césaire of Martinique, French West Indies, and Leopold Senghor of Senegal. Mbiti sees this search for "blackness" in pan-African culture as a useless passion.[27] In my judgment, there is a richness here that theologians, both African and black, need to mine. In doing so we may reach the taproots of our common religious and cultural experience.[28]

The thinking of Africans, according to Basil Matthews, is holistic, and the same is true of religious experience. Neither the dichotomy of either/or thought nor the dualism of sacred and secular is a part of the African's worldview. There is an obvious affinity with biblical faith that informs the whole person and all of life. African ways of thinking and believing may help us cut through Greek dualism and German dialectic and recover the gospel in its ancient setting. This has significant implications for ethics as well as theology. It is of some moment to ponder that in African traditional religion the God of creation and redemption are one.

We will only mention (2) and (3) of Shorter's list: symbolism (which has been treated already) and fecundity. By the latter we refer to a high esteem for humanity and interpersonal relationships. It remains to be seen whether this regard for the human person can be retained as the process of industrialization and urbanization is accelerated. In the meantime, we may gain much from traditional religions to overcome the dehumanizing effects of technology. We will concentrate on (4) and (5) of Shorter's list: communalism and the relation of human and spiritual beings.

Ujamaa, or "familyhood," is descriptive of African communalism. The extended family is at the heart of African community life. Julius Nyerere asserts that in traditional African society individuals exist within a community. He says, "We took care of the community and the community took care of us."[29] There is a vital communion of the life bond that creates solidarity between members of the same family or clan. The fact of having been born in a particular family, clan, or tribe plunges one into a particular vital current, modifying one's whole being and turning it in the direction of the community's way of life. The family, clan, or tribe is a whole, of which each member is only a part. Vincent Mulago writes: "The same blood, the same life which is shared by all, which all receive from the first ancestor . . . runs through the veins of all."[30]

"Because I am, we are" has been used as a way to describe this "vital participation" in traditional African communalism. It has valuable insights to share in ethics as well as theology. Nyerere writes: "Both the 'rich' and the 'poor' individual were completely secure in African society. Natural catastrophe brought famine, but it brought famine to everybody — 'poor' and 'rich.' Nobody starved, either of food or human dignity, because he lacked personal wealth; he could depend on the wealth possessed by the community of which he was a member."[31]

Nyerere, while viewing society as an extension of the basic family unit, suggests that this concept needs to be extended beyond the tribe, the nation, and the continent to mankind.[32]

Theologically, we can see the immediate use of the concept and practice of *ujamaa* in developing a doctrine of the church. The church as a family is present in the thought and life of the early Christian movement. Paul's letters are rich with reference to the church as the family of God and the household of faith. I have written elsewhere in this vein and have found the family image to be a meaningful way to speak of peoplehood for blacks.[33] I have not been unaware of the African heritage as a background. Much serious work remains to be done on both continents. Bonganjalo Goba's essay "Corporate Personality: Ancient Israel and Africa" is highly suggestive of a constructive direction in which to move to make fruitful use of the African concept of communalism in theology.[34]

African communalism has special relevance when we bring the visible and invisible, empirical and supraempirical dimensions of life together. Vital participation in a living community is involvement in sacred life — and all life is sacred. One participates in the life of the ancestors in the life of one's forbears, and one prepares for one's own life to be carried on in one's offspring. Mulago writes: "There is a real continuation of family and individual life after death. The dead constitute the invisible part of the family, clan or tribe, and this invisible part is the most important. At all ceremonies of any importance, at birth, marriage, death, burial, investiture, it is the ancestors who preside, and their will is subordinate only to that of the Creator."[35]

Mbiti is not uncritical of African traditional religion. He is distressed, for example, that African traditional religion has myths of redemption and no account of the eschaton. He celebrates the easy manner in which Africans enter into the spirit world and the fellowship that exists between the living and the dead. He suggests that there might be a renewal in theology and church if we could make creative use of these materials. The sacraments of baptism and Eucharist present themselves as areas in which the temporal and eternal meet. Africans, in their traditional religious beliefs and practices, penetrate into the spirit world through offerings, libation, and sacrifices, thus using the material as the bridge with the spiritual.

Another area in which there could be a breakthrough is the doctrine of the communion of saints. Here African traditional thought and practices may easily bring a renewal into the church's life with regard to the relationship between the departed and the living. Fashole-Luke makes it clear that some aspects of African ancestral beliefs are incompatible with the Christian faith, for example, the belief that no death can take place except by the will of the ancestors. It is his contention that the veneration of the ancestors in Africa and the desire to be linked with the dead can be satisfied by a sound doctrine of the communion of saints. In this statement the living and the departed would be viewed as linked together in an indissoluble bond, through participation in the sacraments, so that earth and heaven meet together and already in this life we taste the fruit of eternal life.[36]

Conclusion: Misplaced Debate between James Cone and Charles Long

In view of all that we have said, the urgency and importance of the task of exploring African traditional religion should be obvious. In the study of African traditional religion, there is an abundance of material for all disciplines of religious studies. The neglect of Africa in religious studies must now come to an end. Much of the responsibility in providing adequate treatment of African religion in the West may rest with black scholars who have their roots in Africa. They have a "double existence," as W. E. B. Du Bois said. They must perform the same task in religious studies that Andrew Young is performing in Amero-African diplomacy.

We have not gotten off with a good start thus far. In dialogues between black and African scholars, it would appear that Charles Long, a historian of religion, and James Cone, a theologian, have mainly aired their own differences in the company of African religious scholars. Theology and the history of religions were contrasted in that setting. Long, who discounts revelation, stresses the study of religious experience as phenomena. Cone, on the other hand, insists on the normative character of Jesus Christ as the revelation from God. If Cone could view the study of religious experience as valid for his interest, Long could open up many doors in traditional African religion for Cone. If, on the other hand, Long could understand the importance of revelation to include God's self-disclosure in all of creation and all of history as well as in Jesus Christ, their views would be complimentary. The dogmatic standoff between these black scholars indicates that they are not likely to facilitate this important dialogue.[37]

While African religious scholars are aware of a distinction between a theology for the traditional religious systems and a Christian theology for the churches, most of them desire to involve the traditional material in their reflections. I believe this is the right direction in which to move. Black religious scholars have a stake in this development. If we are only able to disagree among ourselves, we should step aside and let it happen. But since we do live in two worlds, so to speak, we have the need and responsibility to help make it happen. My desire is to see blacks representing the various disciplines of religious knowledge working as a team with African religious scholars to excavate and interpret this rich religious heritage for all of humankind.

Chapter 11

An Afro-American Theological Dialogue

One of the most difficult assignments for a Christian theologian who has an interest in the worldwide religious phenomena is to find a framework for discussion. And yet in this time of world history, when all humans live in a global village, the task is inescapable. The confluence of cultures, the provisions of science and technology, and many other factors compel us to open up the dialogue to currents of religious life, experience, and thought from all peoples. It is appropriate that those with "roots" in third world cultures should consider this task an urgent and serious one.

This reaching out in interreligious dialogue is easier in nonconfessional approaches. Scholars in philosophy, anthropology, and the history of religions, for instance, can make provisions for two-way conversation with less effort than theologians who interpret the faith of a believing community that makes absolute claims to truth. The fact that any of these other disciplines shows a Western bias does not neutralize the potential for dialogue completely. But theology, by its own self-understanding, finds little room for even a possibility for conversation outside of its own Western tradition. Add to this the excessive baggage of the civilization that has developed in the North Atlantic world, and one has some appreciation of the difficulties involved.

Originally published in *Toronto Journal of Theology* 2 (fall 1986): 172–87.

The case for Catholics differs from that of Protestants, though both have problems with this task. Protestants are often hampered by an exclusive christocentric revelation. Catholics, on the other hand, have held to a belief that there is no salvation outside the church. Of course, there are Protestants who hold a more inclusive view of Christology. Likewise, many Catholics, since Vatican II, have a more open ecclesiology. But the alienation from third world cultures and religions is almost a constant factor. The shadow of colonialism and racism, and often the reality of either or both, stands as a barrier to real dialogue. The present discussion is limited to the Protestant experience in these matters.

The Contextual Bias of Western Theology and Third World Response

Western explorations into the religious history of humankind have been informed by a colonial mentality. This has led to a limited selection of the materials of religion and culture to be examined. Only those characteristics in the thought and experience of non-Westerners that have a similarity with Western civilizations have merited consideration. The fact is that a superiority complex has dominated the scene. This has been reinforced by the evolutionary élan that has been operative in the quest for origins in the history of religions. Religions and cultures have been classified by the schema established by the evaluation of the materials set up by the West.

Philologists, philosophers, and anthropologists, often associated with the British colonial administration in India, for example, discovered Sanskrit and profound schools of philosophy, which made them aware of a whole new universe of thought and religious experience. This discovery of Sanskrit, a language honed to logical and mathematical perfection, is what made the science of language a possibility. Furthermore, the profound thought and mystic expression of the sages of

India must have been a profound blow to the egos of the first Western investigators. It is fortunate that the approach of these nonconfessional scholars was more affirmative than that of the Christian theologians and missionaries who invaded these lands. A real dialogue did take place in which the intellectual and spiritual riches of the East flowed into Western minds and hearts.

Christian missionaries armed with the gospel and informed by the exclusivist claims of theologians ignored these religions and philosophies as much as possible. When this proved impossible, they branded what they found as "heathen." At best they described what they found in non-Western cultures only as a preparation for the gospel. They, the missionaries, carried with them the pride of race and culture and cooperated with the colonial administrators (as some American missionaries have recently aided the CIA) in raping these peoples of their resources and their very humanity. They were confident that God had smiled upon the West and that God would give them victory and an abundant harvest as the Christian colonizers of the non-Western world.

Christians affirm God's providence. For some, this implies that God runs history. We should not be surprised, therefore, to observe that God's intention for non-Westerners varied from that of many Christian missionaries. The *Christian Century,* a popular church journal in the United States, was founded and given its name because of the assumption that during the twentieth century all humans would be claimed for Christ. Most of those who founded that publication did not live to see the last quarter of this century. But we now observe that they did not foresee the impact that the social, economic, and political revolutions would have upon their prediction. In the third world where Christian missionaries expected such an abundant harvest, Marxism and nationalism, informed by an awakening of traditional culture consciousness, have radicalized the situation beyond any vision available at the turn of this century.

At the very time that Westerners had begun to adjust to the social and cultural revolution in Asia, Africa arose as a slumbering giant and presented its credentials on the stage of world history. This was most disturbing because it had been assumed that before Europeans went to Africa for the purpose of colonizing it, there was only the worst form of barbarism. So effective was this propaganda that many blacks and whites assumed that slavery was a great improvement over the African situation. It was believed that in the providence of God slavery had been established both to Christianize and civilize blacks from Africa.

African traditional religions had been dismissed as mere magic or superstition. It was assumed that sub-Sahara Africa (Black Africa) was totally uncivilized. But serious scholarship by historians and anthropologists from within and without Africa has compelled us to take a second look. The evidence is overwhelming that previously we had found what we looked for yet did not tap the riches of the cultures already there.

What has been aimed at in this opening statement is a bold and open challenge to some trends in Western scholarship, especially among Christian theologians and churchmen, which have made our approach to the third world mainly a monologue. We have attempted to prepackage theology in our cultural containers and transport and impose these on the minds and hearts of non-Westerners. Their proper response, as we viewed the matter, was to appropriate our ready-made gospel to their situation. This required of them a passive mentality and a low level of cultural consciousness.

The fact that the conditions for blind acceptance of our theologies and churchmanship are passing has now dawned upon many. History itself and secular happenings more than anything else may force us to realize that the golden age for Western theology and missionary activity has passed into history. What Soki Coe, an Asian theologian, describes as the "conceptualization" of theology is the order of the day in Asia, Africa, Latin America, and the islands of the seas. There is a creative and aggressive mining of traditional cultures and religions for perspectives that will make the gospel speak with relevance of salvific power to the hearts and lives of peoples everywhere. Because the earthly condition of many of these peoples is riddled with poverty, racism, classism, and rampant misery, the gospel is being understood as God's Word of deliverance in time as well as in eternity.

The Theological Impasse

Karl Barth's *Nein* to Brunner concerning natural revelation is symbolic of the theological impasse I wish now to describe. It may be possible to find somewhere in Barth's extensive writings evidence that he changed his mind or that he really did not mean what he said. The fact remains that fruitful discussion with non-Western religious traditions was going on before Barth but that the powerful impact of his distinction between Christianity and other religions eclipsed the important work done by Soderblom, Otto, and others in this important field.

Otto's *Idea of the Holy,* Heiler's *Prayer,* Soderblom's *Living God,* William Temple's *Nature, Man and God,* and similar studies in Holland had opened up a deep appreciation by Protestant theologians for the possibility of a two-way conversation between Christians and religionists of other traditions. Some of these studies are useful only in dealing with religions of the Book (sacred written religious texts), advanced belief systems, and exalted philosophical concepts. The phenomenological studies, however, move into a comparison of any and all belief systems.

For almost a half century this significant pre-Barthian theological tradition among Protestant theologians has been in a state of hibernation, and only a few mute attempts have been made to reestablish that august tradition. Notwithstanding the arguments by pro-Barthians that Barth was not responsible for this state of affairs, the continual reign of Barth through his disciples and the absence of chairs in comparative religions in West German universities provides much plausibility to the conclusions I have drawn.

The most significant studies have been made by historians of religions and philosophers such as M. Eliade, W. Cantwell Smith, W. E. Hocking, and S. Radhakrishnan, to name only a few. These interpreters of religious experience are more appropriately classified as phenomenologists of religion than as theologians. It is worth mentioning that some theologians, such as Paul Tillich, Nels Ferre, John Cobb, and John Hick, have become greatly concerned about reviving the earlier conversation with religionists of other faiths. But it has been mainly nontheological interpreters of religious experience who have kept the tradition of Otto and Soderblom alive. They provide a vital link from that era to the present.

The circumstances of human history, especially the cry for liberation by the wretched of the earth, is going to force Western theologians to overcome the Barth-Kraemer formula in regard to the scope of God's revelation in creation, history, and the cultures of peoples everywhere. I am not advocating a syncretism among religions. I am, however, asserting that the exclusive Christology that is prepackaged in the cultures of the North Atlantic theological community must now become inclusive so that the God who is in Christ as "Emmanuel" can be known and confessed as "Lord of all."

Black/African Theologies: A Look at the Task

There can hardly be a better example in which to contextualize what has gone before than the black/African theological situation. *Black* here refers to the Afro-American. *African* refers to the peoples of Africa mainly south of the Sahara Desert. In pursuing the subject we are aware of continuity and discontinuity between blacks and Africans. After Alex Haley's *Roots* it is to be assumed that most people are open to the possibility that the African influence on blacks is a reality. The African ancestry for blacks is taken for granted here. The consciousness of this in recent years has created a cultural dialogue with all peoples of African descent, including those in the West Indies and South America.

Against this background the dialogue with Africans in the extreme south is restricted. It can usually take place only when Africans from the South can meet in other African countries or abroad. But the impact of the mutual exchange between African theologians and churchmen from South Africa and black theologians is immediate and powerful because of their common experience of racism. Both know that racism is their archenemy. The encounter of the Christian faith with racism in both cases puts dynamic content into the meaning of black consciousness and empowers a deeper understanding of the gospel. The dialogue is highly sociopolitical and has an accusing word of judgment for white oppressors in both situations. Liberation from the reality of institutionalized racism takes priority in this discussion.

The encounter between blacks and Africans in independent nations is more intense at the point of contextualizing the faith in the cultures of Africa. Here the common experience of overcoming the scars of the past oppression can be shared. The minds and spirits of blacks and Africans alike must be "decolonized." Black consciousness as worked out in black theology can be a useful model for developing a sense of pride and self-determination in both settings.

There is a common temperament in African independent churches and black cults and sects in the inner cities of the United States. The common source is African traditional religions and cultures. Thus, historical and phenomenological studies in these tribal religions will cast significant light on our shared investigations.

What is clear is that theological programs, however chris-tological, that are made in Western countries are methodolog-ically and contextually inadequate to interpret the gospel in these new situations. The old wine skins made in theological centers in Europe and America will not contain the new wine. As one who was nurtured in the West, I am not prepared to abandon all that I have learned and start de novo. But as a citizen in the first world with an ancestry in the third world, I cannot but take this theological challenge with all seriousness. Indeed, it becomes increasingly difficult for anyone anywhere to think narrowly and draw a circle that leaves out two-thirds of the human race. A theological circle with such a limited cir-cumference cannot be tolerated in this global village any more than a political one.

African/Black Theology: The Quest

Edward Fashole-Luke helps to clarify the issue in his "Quest for African Christian Theologies."[1] He qualifies his subject by "Christian" and "theologies." He therefore makes it clear that he is not writing a general African cultural theology. This obviously could be done on traditional belief systems. Further-more, he makes it clear that there can be no single monolithic program for a Christian African theology. He correctly points to a plural situation. As a black theologian, I would agree with this outlook and assert the same regarding black theologies and also the necessity to specify the "Christian" content of our programs. The reasons for this agreement may differ, but the description of what is going on in Africa and Afro-America is accurate. It is unfair to the creativity and rich varieties in theological expression in either case to single out one black or African theologian as *the theologian.* African theologians reminded us in a New York meeting that Mbiti is not the only African theologian. In Germany, it often has been necessary for me to say that James Cone is not the only black theologian. This is, I think, not in my interest but in his and that of the many unsung theologians among us. No one theologian should carry this burden. Furthermore, when weaknesses are found in one program, the entire enterprise is suspect. It would be unfortunate to write off either of these theological programs in Africa and Afro-America without a serious examination of an increasing number of able theologians on both continents.

Fashole-Luke's "Quest" also should indicate a profound insight. In 1971 I released (with James Gardiner) a collection of essays delivered at the Georgetown University Conference on Black Theology. This work was similarly entitled *The Quest for a Black Theology.*[2] What is being implied by "quest" in both cases is the stage of progress of these theological programs. It is my impression that black theology in the United States is more developed than African Christian theology, but it is not yet beyond the "questing" stage. James Cone might take exception to this view, but this remains my opinion. As a theologian writing on the subject, I am painfully aware of the incomplete nature of what I have done as well as that of others thus far. My readings of other African and Afro-American writings indicate the fairness of this judgment. This point is crucial. It will take the serious teamwork of many specialists for several years to complete a task so great and so nobly begun.

Other African theologians support the main outlook of Fashole-Luke. For instance, Kwesi A. Dickson writes from Ghana and J. W. Zvomunonita Kurewa writes from Rhodesia concerning the development and meaning of a *Theologia Africana.*[3] What we are saying is that both African and black theologies are relatively new. However, neither is in its infancy, and both have now reached a serious level of development.

These theological movements, on two continents, present a serious challenge to Western theology. They have a significant contribution to make both to theology and the church around the world. My impression is that these theologies are now ready and anxious for dialogue. But they will insist on their contextual validity and integrity of thought. They will not, however, participate in a one-way conversation.

Method and Authority in Black/African Theologies

We are now prepared to take a brief look at thought patterns and sources of authority in black/African theologies. In this section we will reflect on epistemology, Scripture, and tradition.

Epistemology

The problem of knowledge is acute for theology because of the confessional aspect of the subject matter. If there is no confession of faith and no belief in divine revelation, then we are not within the theological circle. We may examine many of the same problems and concepts, but we do not do so as philosophers only. But this does not imply that we do not have a critical task. This is precisely the reason that a theory of knowledge presents such a serious challenge to theologians.

The nature and source of knowledge in theological discourse touches on the main issue between Schleiermacher and Barth, at least as Barth assessed the situation. Barth saw Schleiermacher as moving from humanity to God. Barth, on the contrary, insists that revelation is from God to humanity. How we treat the knowledge question in theology is foundational to everything else.

My own development has been varied. It includes Christian Platonism, neo-orthodoxy, British neo-liberalism, American liberation, and the theology of the social gospel. Ethics and phenomenology of religion are very influential in my outlook.

Cone has been greatly influenced by Barth, French existentialism, and Tillich, to mention some currents in his thought. The
black experience is fundamental in understanding either of us.
African theologians are often influenced by Western sources,
but the African personality radiates throughout their thought.

The issue being raised, however, is whether there are fresh
ways of thinking emerging out of the "African presence" in
African and black theologies. For instance, black consciousness has caused Afro-American theologians to mine the rich
spiritual heritage of their history for the language of faith.
African poets and philosophers have developed the concept of
Négritude. Furthermore, we are exploiting the use of meta-
phors, parables, folk tales, and stories for a forceful language
within which to interpret the gospel. The common language
and mode of thought among peoples of African descent is existential — but also communal. It is therefore holistic. Thought
includes feeling, participation. Basil Matthews of Trinidad
refers to black thought as *soulful, lived* thought.

Professor Nakamura of Tokyo University, in his classic *The
Ways of Thinking of Eastern Peoples,* has treated thought patterns in Japan, China, Tibet and India. A companion volume
might describe the manner of thought among African peoples.
In both cases we are dealing with a tradition in thought that
is not identical with the either/or perspective of the West. The
writings of such nontheological thinkers as Kenneth Kaunda,
Leopold Senghor, and Julius Nyerere illustrate this point.

Just as Asian scholars are searching the classics of the Ori-
ent to find contextual ways of doing theology, African and
Afro-American scholars are creatively at work in their own
intellectual and cultural traditions. What this means is that
theology can no longer be prepared in Europe or America
and merely transplanted in the third world. The Platonic/
Aristotelian tradition that has guided theological reflection for
two thousand years is being challenged head on. Black theologians with ancestry in Africa are participating creatively in this

dialogue. It is unfortunate that most Western scholars seem totally unaware that any of this is taking place.

The Place of the Bible

Biblical interpretation is extremely important in both black and African theologies. One of the first important team efforts of African theologians was to produce the book *Biblical Revelation and African Beliefs*.[4] Among important treatments of the subject in black America, one should note James Cone's essay "Biblical Revelation and Social Existence,"[5] Robert A. Bennett's "Black Experience and the Bible,"[6] and Thomas Hoyt Jr.'s "The Biblical Tradition of the Poor and Martin Luther King Jr."[7] Furthermore, major works by several black and African scholars place special emphasis on the Bible as the textbook for "black belief."

The Bible, for blacks, is a "living book." The creative and providential involvement of God in the history of the people of the Old Testament is a given. A direct relationship through faith exists between God's acts of liberating Israel and the freedom struggle of blacks. In black theology there is no "quest" for the historical Jesus. Jesus is present as a divine Friend. The prophets speak for God in judgment against the dehumanization of the poor and weak. But there is also an awareness of sin, guilt, and forgiveness among blacks. I have written in no uncertain terms about blacks as a "sinning" people. I have further written concerning God's forgiveness of the oppressor who meets God's demands for justice and love toward the needy and the helpless. This not a "cheap grace," for it includes the acceptance of the dignity and equality of all humans and the sharing of power.

We now understand, through our conversation with Africans, why black slaves never accepted the version of the Bible that white slavery preachers and theologians gave them. By instinct they knew that the God of the Bible hated slavery. The traditional religions of Africa have much in common with the faith and ethics of the Bible. Therefore, without theological education, indeed, without exposure to education at all, black slaves understood God to be just and loving. Because of their suffering, the Bible has always been a book of consolation. And because of their understanding of God, the Bible has always been a prophetic book. It has been and still is for blacks an incendiary document against injustices, but at the same time, it speaks of the salvific assurance of each sinner before God.

There is therefore a longing among both black and African systematic theologians for a cadre of able biblical scholars from among their ranks for needed support. Speaking now from the vantage point of black theology, I must say that the appearing of such a group of biblical scholars with the sensitivity needed is not too encouraging. Some are not touched by black consciousness and still repeat their Euro-American sources uncritically. Others are lured away from this mandate by attractive offers that take them out of the movement. Consequently, theologians are forced to do their own exegesis and develop their own hermeneutics and get on with the business at hand. After all this appears to be exactly what theological pacesetters such as Barth and Tillich did and perhaps for similar reasons.

Tradition

Any Christian theology worthy of the name must take the Christian tradition seriously. Black and African theologies tend to do this. However, there appear to have been two traditions — the conservative and radical — throughout most of the church's history so far as the social consciousness of the church is concerned. I have visited the city of Konstanz on the German-Swiss border — half of the city is Swiss and the other half is German. It was here that John Huss was condemned by a church council and burned, a shocking reminder of the reactionary and radical tensions in church history. Black and

African theologians continue to take the history of the Christian movement seriously, but they maintain a critical distance. They find much that they can accept, much that they must reject, and much that they must reinterpret.

E. W. Mshana gives an account of two conferences between black and African churchmen and theologians in East Africa. The agreement of these two assemblies at Dar es Salaam, Tanzania (1971), and Kampala (1972) was to the effect that black theology and African theology are programs of contextualization and liberation, although the situations are not identical. This is why Africans must speak for themselves. Mshana quotes from George Thomas, an Afro-American theological professor, who described black theology as a "religious description, interpretation and expression of the lifestyle and God consciousness of black people, beginning in the African experience in the black diaspora."[8] In sum, Thomas is asserting that black theology comes out of the black church, which comes out of black religion, and that this religion has its roots in the African experience.

Mshana, who teaches at the Lutheran Theological College in Makumira, Tanzania, and who edits the *Africa Theological Journal* observes:

> To hear the African Theology we have to go and listen to the African preachers, laymen, catechists, teachers and ordinary believers in Christ and hear what the Gospel means to them.... We have to look for ways in which the Christian faith is being implanted in African art forms, music, drama, traditional ... dances, stories, proverbs, wise sayings, analogies, metaphors.... We have to go to our African Traditional religion.... We have to translate the Christian truth into African thought forms ... language ... terminologies.[9]

What is needed is for the church and theology to be decolonized. The apologetic needs of African Christians must be couched in African ways of thinking. "Just as Greeks Hellenized Christianity and Europeans Europeanized Christianity Africans must now Africanize Christianity."[10] And thus there is a unity-in-diversity in the contextualization of black and African theologies. But the reading of tradition is remarkably similar. Neither blacks nor Africans are at home with the tradition of ecclesiology or theology imposed on them by Euro-American traditions.[11]

Some Cardinal Christian Doctrines

Jacob Neusner of Brown University has asserted that contemporary Jewish theology finds its context in the Holocaust.[12] I would want to assert that the negative influences giving rise to African and black theology are colonialism and racism — either or both. The positive sources are the rich cultural and spiritual traditions in Africa that persist in the religious and cultural aspects of Afro-American life. It is this mix that provides the setting for a reconception of Christian theology.

Theism

Africans and blacks live in a pool of divinity. The real question has not to do with the existence of God, for there are gods many and lords many. The God question is centered around the nature and character of God. We are often in need of a deeper understanding regarding creation and providence. We are equally in need of insight into God's redemptive plan. But an approach to God that considers only personal salvation at some future time does not meet the demands of faith for a suffering people.

Oppression that leads to ethnic suffering casts the God question in a different context. One has to search for the meaning of life and historical existence while facing the negatives of life. We must ask, Does God care? Does God really "bear our grief and carry our sorrows"? The questions Why? and How long? are often on the hearts and minds of blacks. In a world in which racism is rampant and where, as James Cone says, "to be Black is to be blue," the question of identity, both personal and ethnic, looms large. The issue is not really whether God is the same complexion or hue as we. The color of God is ancillary to the prior question regarding the divine character. We earnestly desire to know if God cares. Thus, questions regarding the creation, passivity, and providence of God move with the drift of our concern for the saving purpose of God. The nature of God-talk or the shape of theism will reflect the circumstances of the existential and ethnic peculiarity of Africans and blacks. Furthermore, the cultural consciousness of Africans and blacks, together with the identity crisis triggered by racism or colonialism, forms the context for the formulation of the theistic hypothesis in black/African theologies.

When pressed to do more for the minorities in the United States, President Carter responded that "life is not fair." Blacks and Africans have lived in this climate in which life is "unfair." What understanding of the Divine will enable us to make sense out of the unfairness of life? What view of God will give us the courage to seek changes in a system that has humiliated us and robbed us of our God-given dignity? No statement on God that does not emerge out of our cultural history or that does not take sides regarding oppression and liberation will be meaningful to the oppressed today. Thus, theistic interpretations coming ready-made from Marburg, Oxford, or Harvard may be edifying to the minds but not to the hearts and lives of the blacks and Africans who are still among Fanon's "wretched of the earth." The task of black theology is to take what can be salvaged from theologians in the North Atlantic communities and translate it into an understanding of God — politically and not merely spiritually.

We need a God who is *being* and not *becoming*. We need a God who suffers *for* and *with* the weak and the helpless. We need a God whose power matches the divine will for good. We need a God whose love is undergirded by God's justice. We need a God who reveals the divine saving purpose *in* history and not merely *above* and *beyond* history. The biblical God is for us One whose holy purpose for human life is manifest not just in salvation history but in world history and through all creation and among all peoples.[13]

Community

Africans are saying that the "communion of saints" must include reverence for ancestors. The formula "Because I am, we are" is a powerful affirmation in Africa. The sense of family extends not only in space but in time. It reaches outward in terms of kinship to the living but moves backward in time as well. Thus, there is a communion between the living and the "living dead."

Whereas, among Afro-Americans, the family system based on blood ties has been severely assaulted by oppression (slavery, discrimination, racism), new forms of togetherness have moved in to fill the void; kinship of a nonblood type forged out of the necessity for survival has developed in the most unlikely place. Large families often adopt more children on an informal basis. Because of shortages in housing and the high cost of the same, many people coming to the city from small towns live in the same house or apartment. In a hostile urban setting, they pool their resources and develop a sense of belonging, a surrogate family. And most of all our black churches take on the character of a large extended family.

It is not surprising that the concept of *ujamaa* from Swahili has been adopted by blacks as a way of expressing this new sense of peoplehood. Black churches, therefore, are seeking an in-depth understanding of their group life as "familyhood." This has significance for our theological statement on the black church. The nature and mission of the church as an

extended family made up of believers in Christ is the context
for a viable black ecclesiology.

Gabriel Setiloane provides an African perspective on human
being and community in these words: "Man is man-in-
community: *motho ke motho ka batho* — man is only man
through other people."[14]

Herein lies the African "tribal mystique." This does not
mean, according to Setiloane, that the individual is submerged
in his or her social environment. It does mean, however,
that "the locus of any individual must extend as far as the
social activity of relationships which constitute it extends. For
instance, the dead are believed to be with the living."[15]

Edward Fashole-Luke, writing on the ancestors, observes,
"We cannot simply say that African ancestors can be embraced
within the framework of the universal church and included in
the Communion of Saints."[16] He continues, "The phrase *sanc-
torum communio* [interpreted] to mean fellowship with holy
people of all ages and the whole company of heaven through
participation in the holy sacraments, gives us a signpost to the
road on which our theologizing should travel."[17]

While black Christians do not seem to hold to this strong
belief in ancestors, there is through their understanding of biblical faith a sustained belief in the reunion of families beyond
death. This belief is dramatically presented on the occasion
of the final rites for a deceased relative. The strong extended
family instincts of African communal life appear forcefully at
the time of bereavement. This common cultural aspect of the
Afro-American connection could be a building block of a relevant doctrine of church and sacraments. It also provides a rich
suggestion for the doctrine of last things.

Christology

While the entire system of Christian doctrine needs rethink-
ing in the African as well as the Afro-American contexts, we

have had to be selective. My final example is in reference to Christology.

My treatment of Christology at the end of this discussion does not indicate a low estimate of the subject. In contrast to Cone, I find this the most difficult to formulate. For this reason I hesitate to broach the subject. There is much latent christocentrism in African theology as well as black theology, and it permeates my writings. But this christocentrism must be inclusive if it is to be viable. The exclusive christocentrism of Cone is inadequate for the contextualization of black and African theologies. This implies serious conversation between theologians and sociologists and phenomenologists of religion.

Cone's instincts are still Barthian at this point. And even if Barth's theology can be called to witness for some ethico-political insights, a serious question is whether his program allows for a non-Christian faith in its encounter with non-Western and non-Christian religious expression to be at the center of both African and black theological reflection. Just as process theologians such as John Cobb are attempting to reconceive Christology in dialogue with Buddhists, black theologians will need to participate in "Africanization" of Christian theology at its christological center.

Any Western hermeneutic will prove to be inadequate for this task. We must look elsewhere for guidelines. While taking seriously Western historical-critical scholarship and the profound theological programs based on this, we need to unlock the riches of black/African spirituality and culture in the way we develop a christological proposal. I accept, for example, the confessional core Christology summed up in D. M. Ballie's classic *God Was in Christ*. For me, the Jesus of history is the Christ of faith. Christ is the center of God's revelation, but the circumference of God's salvific revelation is in all of creation and all of history and among all peoples. God is with us in Christ. God meets us in Christ where we are ethnically and culturally. He is Lord of *each* people and yet Lord of all. Christology is particular and at the same time universal. Christ is not culturally captive in the West. He is incarnate among all peoples in their *Lebenswelt.* When missionaries sang, "Jesus shall reign where'er the sun," they had in mind a white Jesus whose lordship would be over humans of a darker hue in the third world. They therefore in too many instances became colonizers for God.

Bishop E. Bolaji Idowu clinches the point when he asks, "If Christ can speak British, English and American, why can't he speak Yoruba, the language of my people?" Koyama, a Japanese theologian, writes, "There is no handle on the cross." We must now develop a christocentric understanding that is adequate for all people to cry out, "My Lord and my God." And yet the Savior of each person must be understood as the Redeemer of humankind.

Conclusion

The context of black theology is temporally and spatially distinct from African theology. A common ancestry links them remarkably. Here one can claim too much and one can claim too little. What is important is to affirm what we have in common that is mutually enriching and together develop meaningful statements of doctrine for our people through critical yet positive dialogue. To this conversation we invite all people of African descent — those in the West Indies and Latin America as well as blacks and Africans.

We can document from our cultures similarities of religious experience, liturgy, belief, and practice. Racism and colonialism have triggered similar problems of identity and suffering. Therefore, the need for group consciousness and socioeconomic-political change is also similar. Thus, our task of contextualizing the gospel at this time in world history must move forward with haste but with serious thought. Our people are on the move; deliverance is their goal. Those of us who have been called to the theological task must hasten to join them.

Part 5

Theological Reflections

Chapter 12

A Christian Response to Evil and Suffering

Most Christian thinkers have had to grapple with the reality of evil and suffering. It is a "rock of offense" that has caused many to stumble or even fall. Agnosticism and atheism have often resulted from a serious engagement with this subject. It is my view that there is a reasonable (not a rational) faith response to evil and suffering. This faith cuts a path through the bewilderment and mystery we confront. It assures us that the contradictions of life are never final.

The questions arising from reflection on evil and suffering are often discussed so as to justify the justice of God.[1] The goodness and power of God, as absolute attributes, are examined. While I am aware of these profound discussions and will refer to the aspects of the same, my approach will not involve God directly but will focus on human responsibility for evil and suffering. I will move from humanity to God and stress human freedom and responsibility. One may refer to my perspective as Christian humanism.

Another characteristic of the present discussion is its collective outlook. We are aware of the personal and psychological effects of evil and suffering. Our emphasis, however, will be on the social effects of evil and suffering. We will insist that personal suffering from evil is often the result of evil projects, programs, and structures of power.

Originally published in *Religious Education* 84 (winter 1989): 68–76.

Again, we will be aware of the cumulative aspects of evil in the temporal sphere. Human history bears testimony to the sheer enormity of evil in the world. There seems to be a growing aspect to our experience of evil as suffering so that in our time it has become capable of the destruction of humankind as a whole. This will be discussed in keeping with the Western view of time. This is a progressive worldview informed by biblical motifs.

Finally, we are aware of the implications of science and technology in relation to our ecological as well as our social environment. These new means fueled by human greed explain many disasters of this century. The evil forces at work in our period have the means to bring into being the end of human life on the planet as we know it. We turn now to our exposition of these concerns.

Evil as Suffering: The Human Factor

There are many evils that cause suffering that may not stem directly from human agency. It seems reasonable to limit our discussion to the human factor since we seem responsible for so much evil that results in human suffering. This is also an area in which both understanding and action can be combined for the alleviation of much suffering in our world.

As we speak of evil as suffering, we are aware that this is an ethical outlook. It assumes certain characteristics of human nature. These are viewed in a Christian perspective. Against a biblical background, we believe that human beings are created in the "image of God." This *imago Dei* nature in humans implies free will and moral responsibility, personal and social. Also implied is a worthy understanding of God as creator of human life. God is lovingly just. God is a being of moral integrity who loves righteousness. God has a well-rounded moral character, being both "tough-minded" and "tender-hearted." God is the Creator, Provider, and Redeemer of humankind. Being related to God properly leads us to be gravely concerned about evil and suffering in the world. As believers redeemed by divine grace, we are to express our faith actively in the alleviation of suffering among humans in the social world. This includes personal and interpersonal ethical involvement.

We face today a critical human situation. The optimism of the West prior to World War I has abated because of the massive evils of the century. There has been more carnage and brutality in less than one hundred years than in all of human history before 1900. We have majored not only in systematic slaughter on the battlefields but in terrorism and psychological and chemical means of human destruction.

In telecasts, movies, and other forms of media outreach, we have spread the image of the evil side of human nature. Recent generations have been born and nurtured in a climate of violence that has cheapened human life. Many poor young people are confined to a social environment in which violence is a daily happening. We have had our moral sensitivities dulled by a satiation with violent events near and far.

Daily we read, hear, or view events regarding battered women, abused children, and all types of degrading acts of one human being against another. We see new knowledge in medicine, computer science, and other areas of research turned immediately into nightmares because of the evil purposes for which our knowledge and skills can be used. The evil side of human nature is so much before us that a cloud of pessimism could cut the nerve of all moral effort to change our human situation for the better.

A Christian must, I believe, insist that human nature is "a *good thing* spoiled." God's creation is good, including humans. And yet the corruption of the best turns out to be the worst. God's intentions and purposes for human life are noble. Humans are equipped to do good and noble things as a blessing to themselves and all humans. We observe this potential realized in the lives of many people. This is true not only of "cosmic persons" like Gandhi but of many ordinary men, women, and children whose lives have blessed many people. They witness to the potential for goodness that God has bestowed on human life. Thus, our *realistic* look at the human situation need not lead only to despair but to hope as well.

Collective Evil and Suffering

Martin Luther King Jr. tells us of his personal search for an understanding of the love ethic of Jesus that could counter massive evil. King was concerned about the problem of racism and the suffering it had caused his people over hundreds of years in the United States. At first King despaired concerning this quest. Most of the Western interpreters were white males who came up with a good interpretation for personal ethics and interpersonal encounters. King longed for a broader meaning that would cover the major forms of oppression behind group suffering. Marxism and the thought of Reinhold Niebuhr offer some important insights. Marxism, however, was godless and held a too optimistic understanding of humanity. On the other hand, Niebuhr stressed the sin of pride and had some real understanding of the depths of collective evil. Niebuhr, unfortunately, was too pessimistic regarding human potential for goodness. King wanted a realistic understanding of human nature that took sin with all seriousness and at the same time treated sin and salvation with a comprehensive social view. King would not, however, downgrade human potential for goodness. He placed his final trust in divine resources and what God is able to do toward the redemption of human life.

King's discovery of Gandhi and his project of nonviolent resistance gave him the basis for a theological reconception of

Jesus' ethic of love as applied to massive social evil. I believe it is significant that King found a theological ethic, apart from Marxism, that became a means of opposing the evils of racism on a grand scale. King had a good grasp of Marxism, but he chose to reexamine the biblical sources (especially the prophets of social justice) and the ethic of Jesus instead. Cornel West would probably be correct in responding that the method of social analysis in the Marxist ideology could have been useful as King examined "sinful social structures."[2]

We now examine briefly the evils of our economic structures together with the massive human suffering on that front. I will give equal time to Marxism and capitalism. It seems to me that Christians often do not give adequate attention to the economic factor in human life. We teach and preach higher values for human life that include the value of labor, but we may end up with a too limited understanding of the economic dimension of human life. Marxists, I believe, go overboard, stressing the merely human dimension of our existence and investing everything in proper economic relations.

Some Christians take for granted the identity of all life with capitalism and democracy. In fact, the "Protestant ethic" attempts to sanctify rugged individualism and the profit motive. Our God of success comes in as the assurer of prosperity and earthly success for those who are blessed. Hence, religion, economics, and politics are built into our civic religion. When this outlook is supported by the religious right and embraced by the national administration, the misery of the unfortunate masses can become a matter of indifference. Thus, homelessness, unemployment, and great deprivation can be tolerated with impunity in a land of great wealth.

On the other hand, wherever Marxism has been the order of the day, there has been great evil and suffering. Godlessness is a factor. Viewing human life as godlike has some effect in exalting the dignity of human beings. Where there is no god, all things are permitted. Also, where the worth of individuals as persons is not given adequate attention, all forms of suffering are likely. The Christian belief that each person is invaluable is important. When this belief is given up, the individual can be sacrificed readily for the good of the party or the state. For these and other reasons, totalitarianism, genocide, and mass murder are a part of the legacy of Marxism around the world. Marxism does not seem to address the question of meaning in personal life. It does not appear to have a workable philosophy of the state. It does not have an answer as to where we can find resources to deal with the transcendent aspects of human life, which cannot be long ignored. Marxism, like humanistic existentialism, has a good grasp of "sin" but without grace.

Jim Willis, though I don't agree with the full implications of his words, provides a convenient statement to close this section of our discussion. He says: "The Gospel of the Kingdom is the central message of the New Testament. It speaks of the inauguration of a whole new order in Jesus Christ and the establishing of a new people whose common life bears witness to that new order in history."[3]

The Accumulative Dimensions of Evil and Suffering

The accumulation of evil and suffering is an important topic for our time. We have reached a final state of this development unless we decide to arrest the trend. This is certainly the thinking behind the peace movement today.

We must find an alternative to war as a means of resolving human conflict. This is true not merely of major wars but of smaller armed struggles as well. It is not possible to contain the destructive results of limited conflict in a "global village" of economic interdependence. The Persian Gulf is of such strategic importance that the world is eventually involved in what happens in that region. It is difficult to understand why it took the United Nations and the so-called superpowers so long to seek some resolution to that conflict.

The scourge of AIDS, resulting in part from promiscuous sexual relations, has threatened the most wholesome expression of love between men and women. Here is a "good thing," intended by the Creator as a meaningful expression of love between husband and wife, so perverted and misused that we are now threatened on this front with the extinction of the human race. Two powerful instincts are now pitted against each other: *love* and *death*. Like the misuse of free will, this abuse of sex has brought us to the crossroads where a decision must be made. Sex now necessarily has to be given a moral direction or we will cease to procreate or exist. The perversion and abuse of something noble in the Creator's intention now becomes the great curse of the most intimate bond between men and women, even in the state of matrimony.

Again, a Christian looks at this critical situation, the accumulation of evil and suffering, and believes there is still hope. We depend on the potential goodness in ourselves. But beyond this we believe that if we are open to God's grace, we can do even more to change our human situation for the better.

What Science and Technology Have Wrought

Problems of evil and suffering have reached greater dimensions as the result of advances in science and technology. After the Holocaust and Hiroshima, the problem of evil can never be the same. These two events are paradigmatic of all such events that have taken place or are possible. Science and technology have brought great benefits to human beings. The comforts we enjoy are often the benefits these have brought to us. But these two events illustrate the dark side of human nature. They remind us that we are capable of the worst when we use the vast knowledge and means at our disposal against God's intention for human life.

The Holocaust and Hiroshima are events that have opened an abyss of human evil and produced suffering on a scale never before anticipated. We face a perversion of human nature, of human genius and freedom, that is unthinkable and immeasurable. We observe in these happenings, to an astounding degree, the capacity of evil in its collective form. It is capable of searing the conscience of nations and communities. Reinhold Niebuhr spelled this out in his *Moral Man and Immoral Society.* He observed that good individuals can be swept away by the tide of collective evil. They can become unwitting participants in and sponsors of massive evil and suffering.

Here the insights of a Marxist, Dr. Svetozar Stojanovic of Belgrade, seem very powerful. He describes our present human condition as "post-Christian" and "post-Marxist." This situation, in which humans have the potential of putting an end to human history, is not anticipated by either Christianity or Marxism, according to Stojanovic.[4] That is to say, neither movement in its traditional doctrine is prepared to meet the challenge of humankind's total self-destruction. We have the power to self-destruct even by accident as well as by intention. This self-destruction can come by an ecological disaster (largely human-produced) as well as by thermonuclear war. Thus, the human gift of cocreator and maker of history, according to Stojanovic, can literally be used to end creation and history as we know it. We can produce our own eschaton.

As we turn to our final statement, we cannot ignore this Marxist challenge. I see in Stojanovic's concerns the common basis of a tragic human situation, which he acknowledges. But beyond this I see the possibility of Marxists and Christians, as humans, creating a common solution to our possible self-destruction; this is a basis for hope.

The Christian Response to Evil and Suffering

Over against "principalities and powers," the evils of this world, the Bible asserts "a new order." The Christian faith is frank about the reality of evils in our world. It does not bypass the hard questions. History is an arena in which evil powers and structures do their worst to hurt and destroy. Creation itself seeks redemption. We are born in and shaped by a "sinful" environment.

But we are cocreators and coworkers with God as Christians. This is true because God is "author of nature and giver of grace." God is Lord of history. God will have the last word. In the end, God!

This faith is assured through belief in the cross and resurrection of Jesus Christ. Through his cross evil at its worst confronts holiness at its best. The cross represents the highest manifestation of love grappling with the powers of evil. The resurrection witnesses to the power of love that overcomes evil, sin, suffering, and death. The victory of the resurrection is the basis of our faith and hope in a Kingdom (a new order of society) that has come and is to come. The church, as the fellowship of people empowered by the Holy Spirit, is a *gestalt* (structure) to oppose evil structures of power. In this faith and in the cross and resurrection we find the basis of our hope. We believe that where God's presence and power are present, evils cannot prevail and the suffering of the righteous has redemptive significance and power in all of our relations — personal, social, and collective.

Conclusion

In this discussion, we have attempted to discuss only one aspect of evil — that of evil as suffering. We have related evil and suffering because collective evil, as discussed here, is usually associated with great suffering on the part of masses of people. Collective evils stem directly from human agency. If suffering is caused by persons and groups possessed of evil, much relief is possible by persons and groups empowered to do good. Thus, an awesome responsibility rests on Christians and churches, through the power of the Spirit, to be transformers of the evil structures of the present world. With God as our Helper, we can do much to alleviate pain and suffering.

Chapter 13

And We Are Not Saved:
A Black Theologian Looks at
Theological Education

Jeremiah 8:20 is highly suggestive of the status of theological institutions in the area of race: "The harvest is past, the summer is ended, and we are not saved." The prophet expresses grief, in deep sympathy with his people. The calamity referred to is probably a famine. To get the full sense of the passage, we are to remember that "the harvest" and "summer" are two distinct seasons in Palestine. The harvest lasted from April to June; the summer followed as a time for the ingathering of fruit. If the harvest failed, the people could still look forward to the season for fruit. But if both failed, famine stared them in the face since all vegetables and fruits do not ripen at the same time. For example, figs and grapes ripen in some climates as late as September, while some vegetables ripen much earlier. The figure here points to an extension of time for the ingathering of vegetables and fruits. In this case there is no indication that anything will happen to prevent famine. Famine appears to be inevitable. This passage is highly suggestive of the present stage of race relations in many seminaries. Change, however, is possible — and necessary.

Originally published in *Religious Education* 87 (summer 1992): 353–69.

From Optimism to Realism

Time alone will not overcome the incidence of racial imbalance in seminary governance, administration, faculty, and staff. The leadership of too many seminaries remains "lily white." Seminaries will need to take into consideration the history of racist oppression, which has not allowed blacks the opportunity to acquire experience. This is specifically true in the area of administration. Those who select trustees have been slow in seeking racial diversity among those who govern. Black women are especially absent in top leadership roles.

What I am suggesting here is very obvious. If a black person, man or woman, has degree certification, much attention should be given to her or his potential for acquiring administrative skills, especially through seminars and workshops. It is not fair to blame persons for not having experience when there have been few or no prior openings making such experience possible. In some cases blacks may be on the faculty and may have acquired experience and skills in other agencies or academic institutions. These too are passed over, as if no black person will ever be qualified for leadership in theological institutions. It is possible that some white males do not want to be supervised by minority persons, whatever their qualifications. When they make an exception, it is most likely to be a white woman. Preference, however, is given to a white male, even when a black faculty person is qualified and available. It is easier to rely on friendships and the "old boys club" rather than to seek to be just and fair in these situations.

Such racist decisions are usually covered by the outworn statement "No qualified black person could be found." This is prevalent in those instances in which a senior black professor is already on the faculty who might be willing to seek candidates among his or her peers. What is lacking is a commitment to be fair and just in these matters. Seminaries will simply need to do better or they will lose their effectiveness in educating black persons for the ministry. And they also will deny knowledge and cross-culture experience to all involved — faculty and students.

I am privileged to address both seminary professors and administrators as a colleague, since I have been both. At the end of a long career, with involvement in the Association of Theological Schools, I am able to speak with no desire for any position of my own. I also speak to my black colleagues, wherever they serve. Black faculty persons need to be accountable to speak and act for the voiceless and powerless in their midst. There is always the temptation to seek personal comfort and security. But the moment of truth for seminaries has come. Little will happen without pressure from those who care. It is best, at least for the institution, if change can be effected by pressure from the inside rather than demonstrations from the outside. In some cases it may become necessary for boycotts and other forms of nonviolent direct action to be taken. In any event, change there must be.

Black faculty persons may be surprised to find not much consciousness against injustice on the part of black students. On one of my visits to another seminary, I was asked to join a protest on behalf of black students. The dean graciously invited me to attend the faculty meeting with the privilege to speak. I was very uncomfortable when it was clear that the administration had co-opted the president of the black student fellowship to support its agenda, which was the appointment of yet another white male to the faculty. The situation was resolved when the appointed professor decided to decline the offer.

Unfortunately, the course offerings, the lifestyle, and the very interpretation of the gospel in some seminaries rob many black students of any resistance to injustices. Black students may feel so insecure and powerless in some situations as to acquiesce in their own mistreatment. They are so overwhelmed by the knowledge and influence of white male faculty persons that they accept the status quo situation without protest. Again, they are often struggling financially and otherwise to such an extent that they prefer to ignore an inhuman situation in order to be rewarded by a degree. The balance of power is not in their favor, and they know how to deal quietly in such situations in order to exist. Blacks know this from intergenerational experience in a racist society.

White male faculty persons, with their pious paternalism, take it upon themselves to speak and act for everyone. They do not even seek insights from minority colleagues who have the wisdom of experience in these matters. Many black faculty persons are present for public relations purposes, but they are not considered peers who have knowledge and experience to share in human relations. In many respects theological institutions are trailing secular institutions in race relations.

A black law professor at Harvard, Derrick Bell, has set an important example in a similar situation. As a tenured senior professor, he observed that no black woman professor had been appointed to the faculty on a permanent basis. Bell led a protest, with strong interracial student support, to change this situation. What I am suggesting here is that seminaries, among higher educational institutions, should be ahead of all others in the quest for fairness, justice, and human equality in the area of race. In case they are not, those of us who are black faculty persons must sense the need to seek change. But it is so easy to hide behind the cross, piety, and spirituality that we often do little if anything to correct such injustices. If blacks do not address these injustices, as long-time citizens, we may not expect third world students and faculty persons to do so. Blacks must take the lead. If a black law professor has taken such a bold step against racism, black theologians can do no less. We must do so because racism is unjust in the legal sense but ultimately because it is against our understanding of the gospel we teach, preach, and live.

Personal Reflections

Much that I present here is based on years of hindsight. It has now been twenty years since my colleague, James Cone, released his *Black Theology and Black Power*. It has been more than twenty-five years since the National Committee of Black Churchmen released its statement "Black Power" in the *New York Times*. This is therefore an important period for personal reflection. This is a good time to assess where theological education has moved on equal rights for blacks. At least, it is significant for those who have invested so much effort in seeking fairness and justice in church circles to ask, Has it all been worthwhile?

My ministry has been diverse. It has been my privilege to serve as a college dean, university and college professor, campus minister, pastor, theologian, editor of a theological journal, and seminarian dean and president, among other things. Here I write primarily as a theologian and theological educator. Much of my career has been in seminaries as an administrator and professor. As a theologian, I am dedicated to the church and have reflected much of the black experience as it touches family life and the church. As a scholar, I have done much in ethics as well as world faiths. The worldwide ecumenical movement has been within my experience from my seminary days. As founder-president of the Foundation for Religious and Educational Exchange, I have seen that theological dialogue is supported by an effort to bring about understanding between humans around the globe. My concern for justice is not limited to one race. Neither is my interest in scholarship or culture provincial. I therefore cannot be accused of being a "one-issue" theologian. This essay, however, is properly *focused* on racism by one who has experienced and reflected on this social evil.

As we launched our efforts as black theologians and church leaders in the late 1960s, we were very optimistic. We also thought we were realistic. My personal involvement in the

struggle for social justice began in the civil rights period. I
was greatly moved by civil rights legislation (especially the
desegregation decision of the Supreme Court). It was the mission and ministry of Dr. Martin Luther King Jr. that had the
most impact on my life and thought. King's focus on equal justice under the law, his quest for freedom and equality for all
Americans, and his theological/ethical outlook have made an
indelible impression on my mind and spirit. The note of "reconciliation" in my theological writings bears traces of King's
insight. At the same time, I am not locked into the King era,
for the message of "liberation" is obviously informed by Mal-
colm X together with black power/black consciousness and
other developments since King's untimely death.

As a participant in black theology consultations (assisting
in the crafting of early statements on black theology) and as
one deeply involved in interracial, denominational, and ecumenical deliberations, I, together with associates, expected
important changes of empowerment through the churches
toward fairness and justice in the area of race. It appeared
for a time that the "caucus" movement in church assemblies
and the emphasis on "reparations" would yield results of a
redemptive character in the area of race relations. We had
hoped that the gospel would be lived out by all Christians.
This concerted effort had a short life. Black demands drew a
weak response for a brief period because of white guilt. As
a matter of fact, before black theologians could draft a statement on reparations, white church leaders decided that racism
had been given adequate attention.

In some cases committees on institutional racism were
abandoned. In other cases, the agendas were filled with other
issues and racism was sidetracked. The situation in denominational and church bodies was reflected in seminaries. In
the late 1960s and early '70s, the Association of Theological Schools (ATS) took a bold position to improve the racial
situation in theological schools. Its research and publications
reflected such interests. Dr. Shelby Rooks of the Fund for

Theological Education and Dr. Marshall Grisby, an ATS staff person, played a major role in emphasizing the need for social justice in seminaries. But like the churches and church bodies, the voice of ATS is muted. Women's issues (mainly the concerns of white women) and even cross-cultural studies and globalization have overshadowed the reality of blatant racism in theological schools. Thus, it is again time for blacks in seminary education to speak out and be forthright in their witness against racism.

Why Now?

At this time, America again faces a crisis in racial and ethnic understanding. A statement by W. E. B. Du Bois early in the twentieth century is prophetic of the present situation. Du Bois warned that the problem of this century would be the "color line." The focus here is the impact of this reality on theological education. Are our seminaries preparing ministers to meet the challenge of the 1990s and the third millennium? It is indeed unfortunate that race relations between blacks and whites are growing worse when America is becoming increasingly nonwhite. The situation grows more complex as problems multiply. Much needs to be done to prepare future, as well as present, ministers for this gathering storm in racial conflict. How will seminaries contribute to justice and healing in this crisis?

I view racism as a symbolic, even paradigmatic form of oppression in this country. All forms of oppression are related. Rosemary Ruether is correct when she observes what she calls an "infrastructure" of oppression. Jacqueline Grant is even more precise as she describes the triple oppression of black women in her "womanist" view of theology. James Cone reminded us years ago that in America "blackness" is a symbol of oppression. It is unlikely that seminaries will be effective in dealing with other forms of oppression until they face their institutional racism. As a black theologian and educator, I sense the need to focus on racism (of which I am a victim) while standing in solidarity with those who are the object of other forms of oppression.

No people in the United States, other than American Indians, have tasted the depths of deprivation, humiliation, and dehumanization based on race more than black Americans. In some sense the pain of blacks has been sharper because of the closeness of the relationship between blacks and whites, which has been a love-hate relationship. For example, Native Americans preferred death to slavery and have opted for separation and independent existence. Blacks were brought to this country in chains for the purpose of enslavement. All efforts and disclaimers to the contrary, blacks still live in the shadows of slavery and face frequent reminders that they are not fully free and equal in relation to white Americans.

Racism is deeply embedded in the "collective unconsciousness" of individuals and institutions in America. The constant influence of this cancer on the psyche of Americans cannot be ignored or escaped. It must be addressed forthrightly if we are to be a healed society. It has not been easy for me to understand why Jews are so anxious concerning the remembrance of the Holocaust. But it makes sense as they explain that this tragic event must be remembered in order that it may never happen again. We urge Americans to remember slavery and all other forms of brutality and discrimination against blacks in order that these evils may be overcome, never to be repeated.

What this suggests for seminaries is that black studies should not be for blacks only. To the contrary, these courses are just as important (perhaps even more so) for nonblack students. This is true for white faculty and students. It is likewise true for nonblacks from abroad who are recent immigrants to the United States. No third world faculty person or student should study in our seminaries who does not encounter the story of black people and experience some interaction with the black church and community. Without this encounter, whites will not understand themselves. Foreigners will not understand the depths of this problem. It has wounded deeply the psyche of all Americans, blacks as well as whites.

This introduction to America, through encounter with the black experience, is fundamental. Racism is endemic, insidious, and profound. It lurks beneath the surface of all relations that white Americans have with people who are different, especially those who come from third world countries. It asserts itself in cruel form whenever the power and privilege of white Americans are threatened. Without in-depth understanding of foreign cultures and strange settlers in urban communities, blacks often take out their resentment against Asians in their midst. Seminaries need to understand what racism has done to the black psyche. Theological schools, in their policies, life, and thought, are not generally preparing black seminarians for the new challenge.

What we need are schools that are prepared to make a constructive contribution to the improvement of this situation. We do not need to be told that the situation is hopeless. Equal attention should be given to blacks who have made significant contributions to our national life *in spite of,* even *because of,* the experiences of grave injustice and oppression. A theory is not adequate (even if supported by statistics) that does not explain the *exception* as well as the *rule.* Data (however scientifically acquired) can be manipulated to suit the intentions of the interpreter.

A look at the present racial climate in the United States is urgent, especially on our campuses. This is important to seminaries, since their enrollees are college or university graduates. Theological institutions have an increasing number of middle-aged, second-career students, but they also have a considerable number of students who are recent college graduates. We cannot assume that these students leave their racism behind. We, as theological educators, also must be concerned about youth, for the future of ministry will be theirs. Our concern for solid biblical faith and spirituality must not blind us to the burning issues of our time, including the upsurge of racism in society as a whole. Thus, theological institutions need to make sure that ethics, in a holistic sense, become central to course offerings and seminary life.

Though courses in ethics are often listed among "classical" subjects, there is evidence that the ethicist is often viewed as an "outsider" whose insights need not be taken seriously by the seminary community. Evangelical and fundamentalist seminaries need to pay special attention to a balanced emphasis on ethics. Liberal seminaries need to make sure that the fundamentals of the faith are not neglected. Ethics needs solid theological and biblical foundations. Seminaries cannot afford to be indifferent to racial and ethnic tensions. In fact, they must take this challenge seriously. In this time of diversity of peoples and cultural pluralism, a monocultural education is inadequate for ministry. Our seminaries will miss their challenge and opportunity if they prepare men and women to minister only to their "own kind."

It is here that black church theology, holistically understood, has a special place in American theological education. Reference here is to the United States. The black church experience and black theology take the Bible seriously. But at the same time, they also treat ethical and social concerns. These deserve incorporation into the theological curriculum and should be highly recommended for all students. At present, black theology and black church studies are mainly elective and for black students only. These subjects are so ancillary to the curriculum (controlled by predominantly white or European faculty) that even black students often graduate without knowledge of the black religious heritage.

Since faculty advisers do not generally see the importance of such studies, neither do any of the students. This state of affairs indicates clearly that one cannot lead where one has not been. I am pleased to see the increasing interest in third world studies. Globalization in theological education is a project in which much effort is needed. But on the other hand, we cannot fully understand conditions "out there" while ignoring similar conditions nearby. If we first understand "third world conditions" at home, we will have deeper empathy for the same conditions abroad.

White Americans are easily persuaded to reach out to cousins facing economic constraints, say in Eastern Europe. But they are not so eager to address human rights violations and hunger in African countries. It will be the special task of black Americans to make sure that their brothers and sisters in Africa and in the diaspora are not left out of our country's generosity. As citizens and taxpayers, we must see that our nation is accountable worldwide. Our seminaries need a new vision. They are often limited by old-fashioned paternalism, even colonialism in missions. Often the professor of missions is a former missionary who has never accepted the common humanity of her or his charges in the mission field. We need a new theology of missions produced mainly by missiologists who have lived out the mission experience and done scholarly reflection on it. We need a new vision of other religions and cultures around the world. Taking seriously the experience of black Americans will enrich and deepen this new theology of missions. In a real sense black religious experience is a vital bridge between the first and third worlds.

Churches and seminaries have decided to mirror the least efforts in the area of racial equality. Having been an administrator in seminaries, I understand the financial and political pressures that make conformity to the norms of least resistance attractive. There is a budget to be met, and there are conservative faculty persons and trustees to be appeased. It is easier and safer to accept trends in the larger society than it is to witness for racial justice in seminary education.

Even in the heyday of affirmative action, based on quotas and other incentives, seminaries were at best lukewarm in the quest for social justice. Theological institutions did not have to worry about sanctions based on law or government contracts.

If the denominations supporting them did not advocate racial justice, they did not need to seek fairness or justice in the area of race.

Whereas many secular academic institutions have done much to be fair and just in improving relations between the races, seminaries have been involved in double dealing and speaking with a forked tongue. If the word is the deed, as I believe it is, seminaries face a moment of truth. They are due for rapid and radical change if they are to bear any resemblance to the gospel in the area of race. Their record is, for the most part, abysmal. The statistical report speaks loud and clear.

Seminaries have made some progress in race relations if counting black students is the only indicator. But this education can be deceptive if one does not also observe how students fare on the campus or how many graduate and at what level. At my seminary it has been rare to see a black student graduate with honors. The honors ceremony is painful for me to watch for this reason. Other faculty persons do not appear to observe the lack of black honor students as a problem.

One must not let white faculty persons speak for black students; they must be freed to speak for themselves. Paternalism is alive and well on many seminary campuses. Black students are often so demoralized and marginalized that they will not speak up or speak out. In some instances, theological education is "an opiate of the people." This is a sad condition for those who are to minister to the oppressed for the rest of their lives. One of their primary tasks will be to speak for the powerless and underrepresented. Are they being prepared for such ministry if they are docile and cowardly in the face of injustices on the seminary campus?

Change as discussed here is not limited to a body count of students. It would be instructive today to make a survey of seminary boards, administrations, faculties, and staffs to register the real situation. For those who question the truthfulness or factuality of observations in this discussion, this study could be very valuable. It would be a pleasant relief to find out that more progress has been made than I am aware of. It is to be borne in mind that the call here is for structural change, real power sharing in governance, administration, management, and policymaking in all seminary life.

Racism is also evident in awarding tenure for faculty persons. Tenure for black faculty persons can be very difficult to acquire. It has been my privilege to support several black colleagues in the bid for tenure. In some cases I have been greatly impressed by white colleagues who urged me to be thorough and forceful in my report to the tenure committee. But in too many cases seminaries have made it clear that no blacks will ever qualify for leadership in theological education. For seminary education, this is a time of *kairos*. There can be no further hiding behind the cross.

And Still We Are Not Saved: From Crisis to Hope

It is time for white seminaries consciously and boldly to pursue racial equality and move toward fairness and justice in all aspects of community life. It is also time for black faculty persons together with black students to witness for dignity and respect as persons created and redeemed by the same divine Parent who has created and redeemed other humans. They have this right as human beings and believers in Jesus Christ. The equality we seek must include black women as well as black men.

While I will continue to outline the crises I see in race relations in seminaries, I will also make what I see as constructive suggestions along the way.

We need to find a way to prepare more black faculty persons and educators for seminaries. The appearance of the

Doctor of Ministry degree has been more of a bane than a
blessing to black seminarians. During my own seminary days,
the D.Min. did not exist. If it did, my white advisers may well
have directed me to pursue it rather than the Ph.D. or Th.D.
Even so, I was advised not to tamper with philosophy of religion or philosophical theology. It is obvious that I did not
heed this advice. Since the Ph.D. and Th.D. degrees are generally required for faculty tenure and administrative positions
in seminaries, seminaries need to put considerable effort into
grooming capable black students for these positions.

The small pool of Ph.D.s among black religious scholars makes it possible to conduct a search and conclude that
there are no blacks qualified or available. On the one hand,
white seminary administrators and faculty members wish to
shelter their real feelings by lifting up the obvious fact that
black Ph.D.s in theological disciplines are scarce. On the other
hand, they have not been active in encouraging and preparing
young black scholars. The situation will not improve unless
seminaries and departments of religious studies in universities
dedicate themselves to the task of identifying and encouraging
blacks and other minorities to study for these highest degrees.
With effort this situation can improve. Here black faculty persons can make a difference as role models. But the situation
warrants their direct personal involvement.

Again, not only is there a failure to appoint black men and
women prepared through study and experience to leadership
positions in seminaries, but the misguided sense of mission
and the course offerings deny any promises to bring about
radical change. Qualified black candidates seldom make the
"short list," especially for administrative positions. In some
cases their application is simply ignored. In other cases the
faculty leadership is more European than American, especially
German. There is an obsession with German scholarship,
together with a kind of inferiority complex among American
theologians, that may explain this trend. In some seminaries
major professorships and administrative positions have gone

primarily to those who have not lived or struggled through
the deep-seated race problems in the United States. In some
cases these persons may not have any knowledge of or experience in the third world either. No one can lead where one
has not been.

I will try to illustrate the breakthrough in in-depth understanding between blacks and whites with a common American
experience through a personal example. I do not hesitate to
present it here because my white colleague is so praisewor-
thy. Jim Fowler and I were born and reared in the mountain
region of North Carolina. Jim, an expert on human development, and I, an advocate of black theology, have had unusual
opportunities to be on the same programs. But if we had met
as boys, we probably would have been hostile to each other.
It was common for black and white boys to have fistfights or
exchange rocks as they passed each other, going and returning from separate schools of the South. The white boys would
usually call the black kids "nigger" and say ugly things to get
the fight going. Sometimes the black boys would ignore the
insult; other times, if they saw an opportunity, they would
take the white boys on. Happily, Jim and I met as mature
minister-scholars who had worked through many problems
and hostilities based on race. We became genuine colleagues
and friends.

Jim Fowler and I have appeared at many consultations (academic and church events). We were at Boston College for a
summer term, and of course we were together in Atlanta. A
part of our ability to overcome deep-seated racial wounds,
which we both suffered, is due to the fact that our faith
journeys have taken us through many of the same struggles.

It seems to me that the common struggles of blacks and
whites in the American experience must be taken seriously
if we are to turn our seminaries around. This will not happen through paternalism either. Some white faculty persons
feel that because they marched with Dr. King, they therefore would know what is best for blacks twenty years later.

These persons would speak and act for blacks on campus. They are reluctant to empower black faculty persons to speak for themselves. There should also be a dialogue with black students. This is likewise true of women and other minority students. But black women faculty persons are so rare as to be out of discussion. Happily, there is opportunity for an early improvement on the issue of black women on seminary faculties. Black women, who are being denied ordination and appropriate recognition by black male colleagues as well as black denominations, are earning Ph.D. degrees at a greater rate than black men. Yet black women are not so attracted to the D.Min. degree. Black women, denied ordination upon earning the M.Div., often seek a Ph.D. degree. The availability of an increasing number of black women with Ph.D. degrees in theological disciplines makes it more shameful, as we note their absence on seminary faculties. Black male faculty members, therefore, must become bold advocates for the appointment of qualified black women to their faculties. If black men sit idly by, little will happen.

It is not difficult to see that the curriculum reflects this lack of vision and experience in the larger world. If faculty persons are limited to the Euro-American experience, if sabbatical leaves are taken mainly in Germany, France, and England, we may not expect the broad vision proposed here. Again, black Americans are a vital bridge for cross-cultural programs as well as black studies within the American experience.

In some cases seminaries prefer people of color from other countries to Afro-Americans. Persons who have just arrived look like blacks, but they don't think the same way. What is lacking is the long history of oppression and the struggle for freedom in this society. They do not bear the psychological scars of the long struggle, what Dr. King referred to as "the long night of suffering." They are more dependent and more vulnerable in that they are not established and may be seeking citizenship. Hence they are less militant and outspoken —

more peaceful. In some cases blacks who are militant are isolated, marginalized, and humiliated. Blacks who are weak will opt for silence and inaction in the face of injustice. Fortunately, some are strong, having been involved in a lifetime of struggle for justice. These latter will stand up for what is right, even if they must stand alone. At times they may find it necessary to reach out beyond the campus for leverage in order to bring injustices to the attention of the public.

Blacks who are militantly nonviolent are vulnerable, often as a majority of one. They can always be out-voted and may, so to speak, carry their resignation in their pocket. But their life struggle against racism and their convictions will not allow them to be silent as they behold injustices all around them. They feel compelled to speak and act on behalf of the voiceless and the powerless, regardless of personal consequences. The presence of such committed blacks on a theological faculty can make a difference.

Constructive Proposals

Theological instruction intends to prepare persons for true witness through ministry. The goal of seminary education should be to prepare persons to lead in just and fair dealings with all humans. The gospel should lead us beyond what is required to be just and fair by law. We speak of love as a more excellent way. It is therefore shameful that seminaries may be doing less to correct the wrongs in race relations, simply because they cannot be compelled by law to be just. There can be no genuine love that does not incorporate what is just and fair in human relations. It is not sufficient to be against "affirmative action" or "quotas" if you are not prepared to do *more* rather than *less* to make life more human for the oppressed. This is the self-righteousness that defeats the Christian cause. What we need now are deeds and not more words.

In this spirit, I offer the following suggestions. First, there should be an all-out effort to increase the number of blacks in every aspect of seminary life — trustees, administrators, faculty, staff, and students. Black students need role models. If they do not see black persons in all areas of seminary life, they will not be encouraged to aspire to roles that do not appear to be open to them. Seminaries have much to repent of in the poor examples they have set. This observation needs immediate attention. This is something that can be done. It is overdue.

The second suggestion repeats something mentioned elsewhere. The course offerings as well as the mission statement should reflect, mirror, and implement the vision of one humanity under God. Seminaries should not just reflect what is happening in society and church in the area of racial justice, but they should be transformative in their thought and life. The offerings on various forms of oppression should be integrated into the course offerings on racism, sexism, poverty, and so on. Those who earn degrees should be sensitized to these experiences to the extent that they develop a solidarity with those who suffer. In this process the oppressors also will experience real Christian freedom.

Third, seminaries need to provide internships in areas of great need, at home and abroad. These immersion experiences should include nonparish as well as parish experiences. Some examples include ministry to migrant workers, in correctional institutions, in industry, and in social agencies. It is evident that a minister dedicated to vital witness needs to know what is going on in the world outside the sanctuary. The clinical model, with a focus on personal anxieties, as important as it is, is no longer sufficient. There are structural evils to be encountered. These social sins are not unrelated to personal anxiety. In this connection, I should mention internships abroad as a way to sensitize students to structural evils. An immersion experience in Soweto, South Africa, would be very enlightening.

Fourth, I return to the ATS project through Plowshares toward globalization. Plowshares, under the leadership of Bob and Alice Evans, has conducted travel seminars for religious scholars and theological students in Third World countries for many years. It should continue and should be intensified. My focus is on how to make the results of the experience be felt here at home. It is true that some persons need to go to India or China in order to have their consciousness raised. But what does that mean unless they are willing to be involved in ministry to the oppressed in the urban area where they are to serve?

Fifth, we need to give attention to subject matter, especially courses in theology. Seminaries have offered black theology mainly as an afterthought, if at all. It has been made available to appease a handful of black students, if they are sufficiently vocal. But black theology has not attracted many white males. White women have an interest in black theology, but often they want to read their agenda into it. Feminist theology has its own agenda, which should stand. This is likewise true of black theology. It is here that the contribution of black women theologians is most welcome. Black women are critiquing both black males and white women as they attack the triple oppressions of race, sex, and class. The feminization of poverty is very much on the agenda of black women theologians. White women are asked to take a look at the privilege and power that goes along with their "whiteness." Womanist theologians have given equal attention to the chauvinism of black theologians and ministers. Sexism is very much alive in the black church. Black women have altered the landscape for both black and feminist theologies. Thus, the need for black women on theological faculties is obvious.

A Theological Postscript

As a theologian, I cannot resist the opportunity to make an observation. It seems to me that what we have discussed here has a lot to do with theological outlook — that is, how the gospel is understood. This is especially true of seminaries that wear "evangelical" on their sleeves, as if this label in itself were a badge of glory. Such seminaries emphasize the Bible, but what about making life more human? Personal salvation is stressed, but the ethical imperatives of the faith may not be equally stressed. A proper interpretation of Scripture supports both a strong mandate for personal commitment to God in Christ and profound social involvement in ethical issues. This is where I believe black theology has struck a balance. The black experience of the Christian faith has been holistic. The black church has been strong on revivalism and social involvement at the same time. The evangelical-liberal split has no currency among blacks. These two dimensions of the faith reinforce each other, providing maximum affirmation of the personal and social manifestations of the gospel. This outlook of black theology also includes an engagement with structural evils. Thus, it is not limited to implications for social service; it goes on to advocate social transformation.

Finally, those of us who minister in seminaries are responsible for doing all that we can to overcome the cancer of racism in our community life. This can be done only if we are willing to affirm the full humanity of all persons in our midst. To do this we must be willing to select persons according to their knowledge and potential and not according to their race or gender. Only then will we be worthy of the task of educating and sending forth persons to minister in the church of Jesus Christ. Our seminaries face a moment of truth. We can no longer hide behind the cross. The hour has come for deeds rather than words.

"The harvest is past, the summer is ended, and we are not saved." But yet there is time!

Afterword

This collection of essays helps me to see my development and outlook through the eyes of a younger theologian. David Emmanuel Goatley has emerged quickly as one of the most perceptive theologians of his generation. He is also dedicated to ministry. He has been a pastor and professor and has now become a missionary executive. He has had one foot in the academy and the other in the church, and this balance is much appreciated as he reflects on what I have seen as my calling for all these years. My vision also has been anchored in the academy and the church.

In order to appreciate fully what appears in this collection, one would need to go outside of what is presented in this volume. I appreciate the editor's observation regarding this limitation. Nevertheless, for the sake of those who read these essays without Goatley's search into my corpus, a few words need to be said.

This is a response to what has been presented here. This is neither the time nor the place for extensive autobiographical reflections. Briefly, then, my contribution to black theology and black church studies should be viewed in a broad context. This would include what I was about as a thinker before I entered the movement that was the focus of this collection. My work as a philosopher, pastor, and student of world religions preceded the essays in this volume. I also had been a college dean, college minister, and teacher of the Bible and ethics. Ministry to migrant workers made me sensitive to the plight of the poor. All such experiences have enriched my life and empowered my passion for ministry. Though I have not pastored since the 1950s, I have never left the church or the ministry. My vocation as professor of theology at Howard University began with the supervision of field education in Washington, D.C., and Baltimore. But soon the demands of my Howard professorship demanded all of my intellectual and physical resources. I assumed the responsible role of a husband and father of four children. All of these foundational experiences are reflected in my research and writing.

At the time I entered the academy, I was not aware of any full-time African American theologian in this nation. Upon completing my Ph.D. degree in philosophical theology at the University of Edinburgh and studies at Cambridge University as well, I returned to the United States to find most doors closed in seminaries and university departments of religion and divinity schools. My call to ministry did not lead me toward purely academic teaching. My true vocation was that of a church theologian. This was to become my ministry to the church and to the academy. In some ways, I chose what I have been. In another sense, it was chosen for me by racial politics of the period. I am grateful that Howard Divinity School opened to me almost at once. This allowed me to pursue, with vigor, the path I have chosen.

My life has been a "quest" under divine direction. My outlook has been more exploratory than focused. At Howard University I had opportunity to do much interdisciplinary and cross-professional, dialogue-type teaching, which suited my temperament as a person and as a thinker. Howard University was very important as a location for my developmental period. There were no dogmatic restraints on my work. However, my faith claim guided me through many troubled waters, while my spiritual and ethical anchors remained in place. Grants and opportunities for research, travel, and publishing were available. Being at Howard, sometimes called the "Black Harvard," was, in some ways, an advantage. Major academic institutions worldwide looked to Howard for top black scholars. As I considered the opportunities for growth at Howard University, as well as the opportunities for service to black people, there was little that led me to consider other places of service. Only now do I regret the lack of opportunity to groom more Ph.D.s. As I enter retirement, this regret dawns more upon my consciousness. Nevertheless, I continue to read dissertations, guide research, and mentor black scholars throughout their careers. Several of my seminary students from the global community are moving ahead in advanced studies. I continue to follow some of these rising scholars as I am placed on their dissertation committees. Thus, the opportunity for outreach is greater than it would appear.

Early exposure to European study and travel, as well as later study and travel around the world, is reflected in my outlook. This has much to do with my cross-cultural interest. My first encounter with non-Western culture was in Asia. Several of my mentors, including Howard Thurman, Benjamin E. Mays, and William Stuart Nelson, had field experience in India. Thus, I discovered Asia before I visited Africa. Much of my involvement in the Asia experience is absent from this collection. But this is part of who I am.

I want to mention two further background points of interest. Why do I stress reconciliation? Goatley has outlined theological reasons. But there are experimental reasons as well.

First, my world travels and studies of other religions and cultures antedate the development of black theology. Thus, I came to this movement informed by both European and third world knowledge and experience, which had helped to shape my perspective. Epistemologically, I knew the "either-or" and the "both-and" ways of thinking. The mediating theology of John Baillie and H. H. Farmer also made a great impact on my thought. I came to theology with a strong philosophical bias that led me away from any tendency toward dogmatism.

Second, I belong to the generation of black scholars who witnessed the ministry of Dr. Martin Luther King Jr. While I did not and do not accept King's position without critical evaluation, reconciliation remained a crucial theme in all of my reflections. This concern for reconciliation in no way eliminates my passion for liberation. The twin goals of human understanding must interact. If it is true that some persons are more prepared for reconciliation than others, one needs to be willing to accept goodwill when it is found. For me, reconciliation must include justice and fairness. It is always costly. It is not to be identified with sentimental love. I need not labor the point here, as my position is stated in many places throughout this collection.

This collection has been selected with both logic and chronology in view. In this sense, it represents a pattern of development as well as the broadening outlook of my thought. Theology and politics, black theology, theology and the church, theology and African consciousness, and theological reflections are prime examples of both my thought and activity.

Finally, I want to sum up as best I can two foci in my theological project. First, there was a question about faith and intellect: "How can I know what I know (intellectually) and still have a strong faith?" I needed a place to stand that would provide reasons for faith. I have no explanation for my thirst for knowledge. I was raised a "Pentecostal Baptist." There were no college graduates in my immediate family. My father, though uneducated, possessed an unusual mind. He was a skilled person with great mathematical ability. I discovered early that I possessed an inquisitive mind. My teachers observed this craving for knowledge, and it followed me through my early years as a professor. My first two books reflected this epistemological quest.

A second focus to be observed is ethical. The ethical question "What must I do?" guided me through the second phase of my quest. This latter question overlaps the quest for knowledge. I became aware of this by the mid 1950s. I am certain that the ministry of Dr. Martin Luther King Jr. sharpened my desire to search for ethical answers to the many issues to be faced — both personal and social. My formal engagement with ethical theory and practice grew as I moved into the 1960s and '70s.

In the summer of 1960, during a seminar on law and theology, I entered upon this new threshold. Global travel and ecumenical encounters also enriched my outreach. My mentors were important. Mordecai Johnson, Howard Thurman, Benjamin E. Mays, William Stuart Nelson, and Frank Wilson, among others, impacted my youthful life. The annual meeting of the Institute of Religion at Howard's School of Religion brought together the best minds in religion around the nation. As a younger scholar, I gained much from my older colleagues. In this company of black scholars and church leaders, there was a strong emphasis on ethics in the study and practice of religion. These discussions, together with their publication, the *Journal of Religious Thought,* helped shape my outlook.

The flowering of my interest in the ethical implications of the Christian faith came with the eruption of black power/black consciousness. Howard University became an intellectual mecca for this new press for freedom among black people. In addition to the ferment on campus, black church leaders convened several sessions on black theology at Howard University and the Interdenominational Theological Center.

Thus, many forces were at work on me. I found myself drawn into the black theology movement and the activities of the National Committee of Black Christians. I decided to join this new expression of Christianity and provide my own theological reflection on it. My interest in philosophical and theological ethics found expression in this outlet as I participated in this overflow of black ecumenism.

In the meantime, the epistemological quest in the comprehensive area of my theological career converged, and there was to be a cross-fertilization of the epistemological and the ethical in my quest. The essays collected in this book demonstrate this balance.

The "both-and" outlook of my thought is reflected in the ethical emphasis on liberation and reconciliation in my black theology project. In this effort, the mediating temper of my life and thought was sincerely expressed.

As the reader examines this select collection of essays, my hope is that these brief autobiographical reflections will be useful toward a fuller understanding of my theological mission.

Notes

Chapter 1: A Theological Conception of the State

1. T. M. Parker, *Christianity and the State in the Light of History* (New York: Harper, 1955), chap. 2.

2. Heinrich A. Rommen, *The State in Catholic Thought* (St. Louis: Herder, 1947), 137, 288–89. Note that this "Catholic view" is based on the political thought of Aquinas.

3. John C. Bennett, *Christians and the State* (New York: Scribner's, 1958), 38.

4. John Calvin, *Institutes of the Christian Religion*, bk. 2, chap. 2, pt. 12.

5. *Official Report of the Oxford Conference* (New York: Willett, Clark & Co., 1937), 240.

6. Emil Brunner, *The Divine Imperative: A Study in Christian Ethics* (trans. Olive Wyon; Philadelphia: Westminster, 1947), 446.

7. Ibid., 445.

8. Ibid., 458.

9. Karl Barth, *Church and State* (London: SCM Press, 1939), chap. 1.

10. Compare Karl Barth, "The Christian Community and Civil Community," in *Against the Stream* (ed. Ronald Gregor Smith; New York: Philosophical Library, 1954), 20. Cited by Bennett, *Christians and the State*, 46.

11. Reinhold Niebuhr, *The Irony of American History* (New York: Harper, 1935), chap. 1.

12. Compare Albert C. Knudson, *The Principles of Christian Ethics* (New York: Abingdon, 1943), 212ff.

13. Ibid., 214.

14. Ibid., 215.

15. Joseph A. Leighton, *Social Philosophies in Conflict* (New York: Appleton-Century, 1937). Here these theories are contrasted with democracy. Also compare Knudson, *Principles of Christian Ethics*, 215.

16. The phraseology is from Reinhold Niebuhr's *Moral Man and Immoral Society* (New York: Scribner's, 1941). I am not, however, interpreting here his treatment of the subject.

17. Knudson, *Principles of Christian Ethics*, 217.

18. Ibid., 218.

Chapter 2: Christian Conscience and Legal Discrimination

1. Reinhold Niebuhr, "Schools, Church, and the Ordeals of Integration," *Christianity and Crisis*, 16 (1956): 99.

2. B. G. Gallagher, "The American Caste System," *Social Action* (1941): 18.

3. Ernest Q. Campbell and Thomas F. Pettigrew, *Christians in Racial Crisis: A Study of Little Rock's Ministry* (Washington, D.C.: Public Affairs Press, 1959), 27.

4. Ibid., 17.

5. Ibid., 41.

6. Waldo Beach, "Grace Amid Judgement," *Christianity and Crisis* 17 (1957): 2.

7. Waldo Beach, "A Theological Analysis of Race Relations," in *Faith and Ethics: The Theology of H. Richard Niebuhr* (ed. Paul Ramsey; New York: Harper, 1957), 221.

8. "A Hundred Years of Progress," in *The American Negro Today* (London: U.S. Information Service, 1955), 33. Included are several of the legal decisions since 1863 as a basis for the 1954 decision.

9. William W. Crosskey, *Politics and the Constitution in the History of the United States*, vol. 2 (Chicago: University of Chicago Press, 1953), 1049ff. See also Ibid., vol. 3.

10. North Carolina Council of Human Relations, "Prejudice and Discrimination," *Human Relations Bulletin* 27 (January 1960): 2.

11. Waldo Beach, "Storm Warnings from the South," *Christianity and Crisis* 16 (1956): 29.

12. Gilbert T. Stephenson, *Race Distinctions in American Law* (New York: D. Appleton and Co., 1910), 3ff.

13. Clyde R. Hoey, "Speech," in *Congressional Record*, 81st Congress, First Session (1949), 4.

Chapter 3: Black Theology and the Theological Revolution

1. Harvey Cox, "Secular Search for Religious Experiences," *Theology Today* 25, no. 3 (October 1968): 321.

2. Ibid., 320.

3. Joseph R. Brandt, *Why Black Power?* (New York: Friendship Press, 1968), 120.

4. Vincent Harding, "The Religion of Black Power," in *The Religious Situation: 1968* (ed. Donald R. Cutler; Boston: Beacon, 1968), 9.

5. Ibid., 9–10.

6. Thomas W. Ogletree, "From Anxiety to Responsibility: The Shifting Focus of Theological Reflection," in *New Theology*, no. 6 (ed. Martin E. Marty and Dean G. Peerman; New York: Macmillan, 1969), 64–65.

7. Quoted in "Black Theology," a statement of the National Committee of Black Churchmen, Atlanta, June 1969.

8. Charles H. Long, "The Death of God: Creativity or Decadence," *Criterion* 7, no. 3 (spring 1968): 17.

9. Ibid., 17–18.

10. Robert McAfee Brown, "How My Mind Has Changed," *Christian Century* (14 January 1970): 45.

11. Martin E. Marty and Dean G. Peerman, eds., *New Theology*, no. 1 (New York: Macmillan, 1966), 34–43.

12. Richard Shaull, "Liberal and Radical in an Age of Discontinuity," *Christianity and Crisis* 29, no. 23 (5 January 1970): 342.

13. Reinhold Niebuhr, "The Presidency and the Irony of American History," *Christianity and Crisis* 30, no. 6 (13 April 1970): 70.

14. Ibid., 70–72.

15. Gabriel Fackre, "Realism and Vision," *Christianity and Crisis* 30, no. 6 (13 April 1970): 73.

16. Ibid., 77.

17. Richard Wilson, "Nixon's Big Gamble," *Look* (5 May 1970): 21–25.

18. Harvey Cox, "Preventative War against the Black Panthers," *Christianity and Crisis* 29, no. 23 (3 January 1970): 338.

19. Ibid., 337.

Chapter 4: Christian Liberation Ethics

1. William C. Settles Jr., "African Religious Survivals as Factors in American Slave Revolts," *Journal of Negro History* 56 (1971): 97.

2. Ibid., 103–4.

3. Charles H. Long, "Perspectives for a Study of Afro-American Religion in the United States," *History of Religions* (August 1971): 66.

4. Robert Bennett, "Black Experience and the Bible," *Theology Today* 27 (1971): 426.

5. Ibid., 433.

6. Jürgen Moltmann, "The Theological Basis of Human Rights," *The Reformed World* 34 (1976): 51–52.

7. Glenn R. Bucher, "Social Gospel Christianity and Racism," *Union Seminary Quarterly Review* 27 (1973): 153.

8. Quoted in Benson Y. Landis, *A Rauschenbusch Reader* (New York: Harper, 1957), 97.

9. Reinhold Niebuhr, *Moral Man and Immoral Society* (New York: Scribner's, 1960), xii.

10. Ibid., 252.

11. Ibid., 253.

12. James M. Gustafson, *Christian Ethics and the Community* (Philadelphia: Pilgrim Press, 1971).

13. Martin Luther King Jr., *Stride toward Freedom: The Montgomery Story* (New York: Harper, 1958), 102.

Chapter 5: Black Religion

1. E. Franklin Frazier, *The Negro Church in America* (New York: Schocken Books, 1963), 5–6.

2. Ibid., 9.

3. W. E. B. Du Bois, "Of the Faith of the Fathers," in *The Black Church in America* (ed. H. M. Nelson et al.; New York: Basic Books, 1971), 30–31.

4. Ibid., 31.

5. W. E. B. Du Bois, *The Souls of Black Folk: Essays and Sketches* (Greenwich, Conn.: Fawcett, 1968).

6. Paul Radin, *God Struck Me Dead* (Philadelphia: Pilgrim Press, 1969), vii–xi.

7. Du Bois, "Of the Faith of the Fathers," 30–31.

8. "Black Theology," a statement of the National Committee of Black Churchmen, in *Journal of Religious Education* of the A.M.E. Church (March 1970): 3.

9. Ibid.

10. LeRoi Jones, *Blues People: Negro Music in White America* (New York: Morrow, 1963), 34.

11. Ibid., 38.

12. James Weldon Johnson and J. Rosamond Johnson, "Lift Every Voice and Sing" (New York: Edward B. Marks Music Co.), stanza 3.

Chapter 6: A Black Ecclesiology of Involvement

1. R. H. Fuller, "Church," in *A Theological Word Book of the Bible* (ed. Alan Richardson; New York: Macmillan, 1953), 49.

2. John Henrik Clarke in *Black Fire* (ed. LeRoi Jones and Larry Neal; New York: Morrow, 1969), 18.

Chapter 7: The Status of Black Catholics

1. Benjamin J. Blied, *Catholics and the Civil War* (Milwaukee, 1945), 13.

2. Frederick Douglass, *Narrative of the Life of an American Slave* (1845; repr., Cambridge: Harvard University Press, 1960).

3. Stallings has received abundant press coverage for his movement. More than twenty articles and editorials on his movement appeared in the *Washington Post* and the *Washington Times* between July and August of 1989. In addition, there was significant coverage nationwide, for example, in *The Charlotte Observer,* 9 July 1989. The founding of the Imani Temple led to much coverage of the plight and aspirations of black Catholics. There was a media blitz.

4. Marjorie Hyer, "Drive Racism from Church, O'Connor Tells Black Catholics," *Washington Post,* 5 August 1989, sec. A2.

5. Marjorie Hyer, "Prelates to Study Need for African American Rite," *Washington Post,* 26 July 1989, sec. A16.

6. Jacqueline Trescott, "Black Priests at a Crossroads," *Washington Post,* 8 August 1989, sec. B1.

7. Peter Steinfels, "Shortage of Entrants to the Clergy Causing Alarm for U.S. Religions," *New York Times,* 9 July 1989, sec. 1, p. 22.

8. Trescott, "Black Priests at a Crossroads," sec. B1.

9. Edward K. Braxton, "Reflections from a Theological Perspective," in *This Far by Faith* (Washington, D.C.: National Office of Black Catholics, 1977), 58–75.

10. James H. Cone, *Speaking the Truth* (Grand Rapids: Eerdmans, 1986), 50–60.

11. "Reflections of a Pastor: 'To Father Stallings, I Say Come Home,' " *Washington Post,* OpEd by James Cardinal Hickey, 13 July 1989, sec. A23.

12. Roger Cardinal Etchegaray, "The Church and Religion" (Rome: The Vatican, 1988).

Chapter 8: African Religion and Social Consciousness

1. John S. Mbiti, *African Religions and Philosophy* (New York: F. A. Praeger, 1969), 6–7.

2. Ibid., 7–8.

3. Ibid., 8.

4. Ibid., 9.

5. Ibid., 9–10.

6. Jack Mendelsohn, *God, Allah and Ju Ju: Religion in Africa Today* (Boston: Beacon, 1962), 63–64.

7. Mbiti, *African Religions*, 10.

8. Placide Tempels, *Bantu Philosophy* (Paris: Presence Africaine, 1969), 23.

9. Mbiti, *African Religions*, 10.

10. Janheinz Jahn, *Muntu: An Outline of the New African Culture* (trans. Marjorie Grene; New York: Grove Press, 1961), 20.

11. Bronislaw Malinowski, *The Dynamics of Cultural Change* (New Haven: Yale University Press, 1945), 24, 153–61.

12. Mbiti, *African Religions*, 10.

13. John S. Mbiti, "Christianity and Traditional Religions in Africa," *International Review of Mission* 59, no. 236 (October 1970): 430–31.

14. Jack Mendelsohn, *God, Allah and Ju Ju: Religion in Africa Today* (Boston: Beacon, 1962).

15. Noel Q. King, *Religions of Africa: A Pilgrimage into Traditional Religions* (New York: Harper, 1970). This work is informed by the discipline of history of religion and is especially noteworthy for its more sympathetic approach. It is more critical than Taylor's earlier work.

16. Kenneth Morgan, ed., *The Religion of the Hindus* (New York: Ronald Press, 1953); *The Path of Buddha* (New York: Ronald Press, 1956); *Islam: The Straight Path* (New York: Ronald Press, 1958).

17. Christian Gaba, "Contemporary Research in African Traditional Religion," *The Ghana Bulletin of Theology* 3, no. 4 (June 1968): 4–5.

18. Mbiti, *African Religions*, 1.

19. See Yosef ben-Jochannan, *African Origins of the Major Western Religions* (New York: African-American Heritage Series, 1970); Helmer Ringgren and Åke V. Ström, *Religions of Mankind: Today and Yesterday* (ed. J. C. G. Greig.; trans. Neils L. Jensen; Philadelphia: Fortress, 1967), 7–21; and Frank M. Snowden Jr., *Blacks in Antiquity* (Cambridge: Harvard University Press, 1970).

20. Vittorio Lanternari, *The Religions of the Oppressed* (New York: New American Library, 1965), 18–62.

21. John V. Taylor, *The Primal Vision: Christian Presence among African Religion* (Philadelphia: Fortress, 1963), 93.

22. Ringgren and Strom, *Religions of Mankind*, 14–18.

Chapter 9: Africanisms and Spiritual Strivings

1. Robert L. Shinn, "On the Way to Desegregation," *Christianity and Crisis* 30, no. 5 (30 March 1970): 53. Compare Whitney Young, "Working Together for Our Common Humanity," *Religious Education* 65, no. 2 (March–April 1970): 143.

2. Carter G. Woodson, *The African Background Outlined* (New York: Negro Universities Press, 1968), 390.

3. Andrew Billingsley, *Black Families in White America* (Englewood Cliffs, N.J.: Prentice-Hall, 1968), 10.

4. Theodore Draper, "The Fantasy of Black Nationalism," *Commentary* (September 1969): 27–54.

5. Joseph A. Tillinghast, *The Negro in Africa and America* (1902; reprint, New York: Negro Universities Press, 1968), 46–79. Compare Woodson, *African Background Outlined,* for a worthy appreciation of the Black man's past.

6. Charles H. Long, "The Black Reality: Toward a Theology of Freedom," *Criterion* 7, no. 2 (spring–summer 1969): 3.

7. E. Franklin Frazier, *The Negro Church in America* (New York: Schocken Books, 1963), 9–11.

8. Ibid., 12–19.

9. LeRoi Jones, *Blues People: Negro Music in White America* (New York: Morrow, 1963), 34.

10. Ibid.

11. Ibid., 36–37.

12. Ibid., 38.

13. Ibid., 39.

14. Quoted in Jones, *Blues People,* 39.

15. Ibid., 40. Concerning the origins of black Americans, see several essays in August Meier and Elliott Rudwick, eds., *The Making of Black America,* vol. 1 (New York: Atheneum, 1969), 3–87. See Meyer Fortes, "Oedipus and the Job in West African Religion," in *Anthropology of Folk Religion* (ed. Charles M. Leslie; New York: Vintage, 1960), 5–49. Compare Placide Tempels, "Concepts of Wickedness in Bantu Philosophy," in *African Heritage: Intimate Views of the Black Africans from Life, Lore, and Literature* (ed. Jacob Drachler; New York: Crowell Collins Press, 1963), 258–266; and Miles Mark Fisher, *Negro Slave Songs in the United States* (New York: Russell & Russell, 1968), 1–26.

16. John Hope Franklin, *From Slavery to Freedom,* 3d ed. (New York: Vintage, 1969), 40–41.

17. Ibid., 41. Some sociologists, such as Edward B. Reuter and Robert E. Park, see no traces of the African background among American Negroes. E. Franklin Frazier's negative position does not appear to go that far. On the other hand, Carter G. Woodson and Melville J. Herskovitz insist on the survival of the African cultural heritage among American Negroes. Franklin conducts his own investigation, cautiously following Herskovitz. See Melville J. Herskovitz, *The Myth of the Negro Past* (Boston: Beacon, 1969), 207–60.

18. Ruby F. Johnson, *The Development of Negro Religion* (New York: Philosophical Library, 1954), xx.

19. Ibid., 17.

20. Ibid., xxi.

21. Viktor Frankl, *Man's Search for Meaning* (New York: Washington Square Press, 1963), 12–14, 16.
22. Ibid., 35.
23. Ibid., 36.
24. Clifton H. Johnson, ed., *God Struck Me Dead: Voices of Ex-Slaves* (Philadelphia: Pilgrim Press, 1969), 24–28.
25. Frankl, *Man's Search*, 54.
26. Ibid., 56–57.
27. James Weldon Johnson and J. Rosamond Johnson, "Lift Every Voice and Sing" (New York: Edward B. Marks Music Co.), stanza 2.
28. Johnson, *Development of Negro Religion*, xxi.
29. Joseph R. Washington Jr., *Black Religion* (Boston: Beacon, 1964).
30. Ibid., 161.
31. Ibid., 289.
32. Johnson and Johnson, "Lift Every Voice," stanza 3.

Chapter 10: Traditional African Religion and Christian Theology

1. Aylward Shorter, *African Christian Theology* (Maryknoll, N.Y.: Orbis, 1977), 11–14.
2. "Engagement," a statement issued by the All-Africa Conference of Churches, Nairobi, 1969.
3. John S. Mbiti, *New Testament Eschatology in an African Background* (New York: Oxford, 1971), 189–90.
4. E. Bolaji Idowu, *African Traditional Religion: A Definition* (Maryknoll, N.Y.: Orbis, 1973), xi.
5. Shorter, *African Christian Theology*, 24–25.
6. E. Bolaji Idowu, "Introduction," in *Biblical Revelation and African Beliefs* (ed. Kwesi A. Dickson and Paul Ellingworth; Maryknoll, N.Y.: Orbis, 1969), 10.
7. Shorter, *African Christian Theology*, 25.
8. Ibid., 26.
9. John S. Mbiti, "Eschatology," in *Biblical Revelation*, 159–62.
10. Ibid., 163. My estimate of Mbiti's contribution is not uncritical. Most African religious scholars are severe critics of Mbiti's proposal. Few, if any, have been able to provide a constructive alternative. I encourage and welcome their contribution to this subject.
11. Charles H. Long, *Alpha, the Myths of Creation* (New York: George Braziller, 1963), 11.
12. Ibid., 12.
13. Ibid.
14. Ibid., 13–14.

15. Ibid., 18.

16. Ibid., 18–19.

17. Charles H. Long, "Structural Similarities and Dissimilarities in Black and African Theologies," *Journal of Religious Thought* 32, no. 2 (1975): 9–24.

18. Osadolor Imasogie, "African Traditional Religion and Christian Faith," *Review and Expositor* 70, no. 3 (summer 1973): 289–90.

19. Peter Bolink, "God in Traditional African Religion: A 'Deus Otiosus?'" *Journal of Theology for Southern Africa,* no. 5 (December 1973): 27–28.

20. Ibid., 28.

21. John S. Mbiti, "African Names of God," *Orita* 6, no. 1 (June 1972): 5.

22. Ibid., 14. Compare E. Bolaji Idowu, "God," in *Biblical Revelation,* 9–28.

23. Shorter, *African Christian Theology,* 34–36.

24. Basil S. Matthews, "Whole-Making: Tagore and Thurman," *Journal of Religious Thought* 34, no. 2 (fall–winter 1977–78): 38–39.

25. From "Modern Pedagogy," an address to the Senegal National Scholarships Convention, 7 July 1971.

26. Leopold Sédar Senghor, "Spirit of Civilization or the Laws of African Negro Culture," First Conference of Negro Writers and Artists, Paris, 1956.

27. John S. Mbiti, *African Religions and Philosophy* (Garden City, N.Y.: Doubleday, 1970), 351–53.

28. Edward A. Jones, *Voice of Negritude* (Valley Forge, Pa.: Judson Press, 1971), 13–17.

29. Julius K. Nyerere, *Ujamaa: Essays on Socialism* (Nairobi: Oxford, 1968), 7.

30. Vincent Mulago, "Vital Participation," in *Biblical Revelation,* 139.

31. Nyerere, *Ujamaa,* 3–4.

32. Ibid., 12.

33. "A Black Ecclesiology of Involvement," *Journal of Religious Thought* 32, no. 1 (1975): 36–47.

34. Bonganjalo Goba, "Corporate Personality: Ancient Israel and Africa," in *The Challenge of Black Theology in South Africa* (ed. Basil Moore; Atlanta: John Knox, 1974), 65–73.

35. Mulago, "Vital Participation," *Biblical Revelation,* 139.

36. Edward W. Fashole-Luke, "Ancestor Veneration and the Communion of Saints," in *New Testament Christianity for Africa and the World* (ed. Mark E. Glasswell and Edward W. Fashole-Luke; London: SPCK, 1974), 220.

37. Cf. James H. Cone, "Report — Black and African Theologies: A Consultation," *Christianity and Crisis* (3 March, 1975): 50–52. Cone's

essay "Black Theology and the Black Church," *CrossCurrents* 27, no. 2 (summer 1977), 147–56. Charles H. Long, "Perspectives for a Study of Afro-American Religion in the United States," *History of Religions* 2, no. 1 (August 1971): 54–66. Long, "Structural Similarities," 9–24.

Chapter 11: An Afro-American Theological Dialogue

1. Edward W. Fashole-Luke, "The Quest for African Christian Theologies," *Scottish Journal of Theology* 29 (1976): 159–75.

2. James J. Gardiner and J. Deotis Roberts, eds., *The Quest for a Black Theology* (Philadelphia: Pilgrim Press, 1971).

3. Kwesi A. Dickson, "Towards a Theological Africana," in *New Testament Christianity for Africa and the World* (ed. Mark E. Glasswell and Edward W. Fashole-Luke; London: SPCK, 1974), 199–207. Compare John W. Z. Kurewa, "The Meaning of African Theology," *Journal of Theology for Southern Africa* 11 (1975): 32–42.

4. Kwesi A. Dickson and Paul Ellingworth, eds., *Biblical Revelation and African Beliefs* (Maryknoll, N.Y.: Orbis, 1969).

5. James H. Cone, "Biblical Revelation and Social Existence," *Interpretation* 28 (1974): 422–40.

6. Robert A. Bennett, "Black Experience and the Bible," *Theology Today* 27 (1971): 422–33.

7. Thomas Hoyt Jr., "The Biblical Tradition of the Poor and Martin Luther King Jr.," *ITC Journal* 4 (1977): 12–31.

8. Quoted in E. W. Mshana, "The Challenge of Black Theology and African Theology," *Africa Theological Journal* 5 (December 1972): 22.

9. Ibid., 21.

10. Ibid., 26.

11. Ibid., 28.

12. In a lecture presented to the Faculty of Theology at the University of Tübingen, 11 October 1977.

13. See Peter Bolink, "God in Traditional African Religion," *Journal of Theology for Southern Africa* 5 (1973): 19–28. Compare James H. Cone, *God of the Oppressed* (New York: Seabury Press, 1975).

14. Gabriel M. Setiloane, "Confessing Christ Today, from One African Perspective: Man and Community," *Journal of Theology for Southern Africa* 3 (1975): 31.

15. Ibid., 33.

16. Edward W. Fashole-Luke, "Ancestor Veneration and the Communion of Saints," in *New Testament Christianity for Africa and the World*, 214.

17. Ibid.

Chapter 12: A Christian Response to Evil and Suffering

1. Among religious thinkers who have treated this problem in depth, John Hick and Paul Ricoeur are outstanding representatives. Hick has treated the problem in his *Evil and the God of Love* (New York: Harper, 1966). Compare his intense discussion in *Encyclopedia of Philosophy,* vol. 3 (London: Collier-Macmillan, 1967), 136–141 (includes bibliography).

While Hick approaches the problem as a philosopher-theologian, Ricoeur's approach is more that of a philosopher and historian of religion. Ricoeur is more concerned with myth and symbolism. He goes beyond the Western tradition into Hindu and Buddhist religious traditions. His *Symbolism of Evil* (Boston: Beacon, 1967) is a definitive study. Compare his article on "evil" in *Encyclopedia of Religion,* vol. 5 (New York: Macmillan, 1987), 199–208.

In fairness to Hick, his discussion goes into Hinduism in a later work. He seeks the vindication of the love of God in the future, in the *eschaton* rather than in *creation*. Therefore "reincarnation" has a special appeal. See Hick, *Death and Eternal Life* (New York: Harper, 1976).

2. See Martin Luther King Jr., *Stride toward Freedom: The Montgomery Story* (New York: Harper, 1958). Compare Cornel West, *Prophesy Deliverance! An Afro-American Revolutionary Christianity* (Philadelphia: Westminster, 1986).

3. Jim Wallis, *Agenda for Biblical People* (New York: Harper, 1976), 3.

4. Svetozar Stojanovic, paper and discussion at a Marxist-Christian dialogue, Granada, Spain, August 1988.

Selected Bibliography of Works by J. Deotis Roberts

Books

Faith and Reason: A Comparative Study of Pascal, Bergson and James. Boston: Christopher, 1962.

From Puritanism to Platonism in Seventeenth Century England. The Hague: Martinus Nijhoff, 1968.

Liberation and Reconciliation: A Black Theology. Philadelphia: Westminster, 1971. Revised, Maryknoll, N.Y.: Orbis, 1994.

Coeditor with James J. Gardiner, *Quest for a Black Theology.* Philadelphia: Pilgrim Press, 1971.

Extending Redemption and Reconciliation. St. Louis: Christian Board of Publication, 1973.

A Black Political Theology. Philadelphia: Westminster, 1974.

The Roots of a Black Future. Philadelphia: Westminster, 1980.

A Theological Commentary on the Sullivan Principles. Philadelphia: International Council of Equality of Opportunity, 1980.

Christian Beliefs. Atlanta: John Colton & Associates, 1981. Revised, Silver Spring, Md.: J. Deotis Roberts Press, 2000.

Black Theology Today. Lewiston, N.Y.: Edwin Mellon Press, 1983.

The Prophethood of Black Believers: An African American Political Theology for Ministry. Louisville, Ky.: Westminster John Knox, 1994.

Africentric Christianity: A Theological Appraisal for Ministry. Valley Forge, Pa.: Judson, 2000.

Essays

"The American Negro's Contribution to Religious Thought." Pages 75–108 in *The Negro Impact on Western Civilization.* Edited by Joseph S. Roucek and Thomas Kiernan. New York: Philosophical Library, 1970. Repr. from *Swarthmore College Bulletin* Alumni Issue (October 1970): 7–15.

"Black Consciousness in Theological Perspective." Pages 62–81 in *Quest for a Black Theology*. Edited by James J. Gardiner and J. Deotis Roberts. Philadelphia: Pilgrim Press, 1971.

"The Forgiveness of Sins." In *Christian Theology: A Case Study Approach*. Edited by Robert A. Evans and Thomas D. Parker. New York: Harper, 1976.

"Afflicted, but Not Defeated." Pages 64–67 in *Preaching the Gospel*. Edited by Henry J. Young. Philadelphia: Fortress Press, 1976.

"Het woord van verzoening." Pages 53–68 in *Om Het Zwart Te Zeggen*. Kampen, Netherlands: J. H. Kok, 1976.

"Liberation Theism." Pages 233–46 in *Black Theology II*. Edited by Calvin E. Bruce and William R. Jones. Lewisburg, Pa: Bucknell University Press, 1978.

"Traditional African Religions and Christianity." Pages 92–115 in *Towards a Global Congress of World Religions*. Edited by Warren Lewis. New York: Rose of Sharon Press, 1978.

"Models of Christian Discipleship: An African/Afro-American Perspective." Pages 171–76 in *Christ's Lordship and Religious Pluralism*. Edited by Gerald H. Anderson and Thomas F. Stransky. Maryknoll, N.Y.: Orbis, 1981.

"A Creative Response to Racism." Pages 35–41 in *The Church and Racism*. Edited by Gregory Baum and John Coleman. New York: Seabury Press, 1982.

"Black Theology in Historic Perspective." Pages 121–34 in *Religionen Geschicte Oekumene*. Edited by Rainer Flasche and Erich Gelback. Leiden, Netherlands: E. J. Brill, 1982.

"Hermeneutics: History and Providence." Pages 315–26 in *Hermeneutics and Horizons: The Shape of the Future*. Edited by Frank K. Flinn. New York: Rose of Sharon Press, 1982.

"Thurman's Contributions to Black Religious Thought." Pages 306–10 in *God and Human Freedom: A Festschrift in Honor of Howard Thurman*. Edited by Henry J. Young. Richmond, Ind.: Friends United Press, 1983.

"Compassion, Vision and Solidarity." Pages 306–10 in *Conflict and Context*. Edited by Mark Lau Branson and C. Rene Padilla. Grand Rapids: Eerdmans, 1986.

"Faith in God Confronts Collective Evils." Pages 15–27 in *The Search for Faith and Justice in the Twentieth Century*. Edited by Gene G. James. New York: Paragon House, 1987.

"Religio-Ethical Reflections upon the Experiential Components of a Philosophy of Black Liberation." Pages 249–69 in *African American Religious Studies: An Interdisciplinary Anthology*. Edited by Gayraud S. Wilmore. Durham: Duke University Press, 1989.

"Bernard L. Ramm's Apologetic Use of Philosophy." Pages 43–45 in *Perspectives on Theology in the Contemporary World: Essays in Honor of Bernard Ramm*. Edited by Stanley J. Grenz. Macon: Mercer University Press, 1990.
"Common Themes: Black Theology and Minjung Theology." Pages 405–9 in *Black Theology: A Documentary History*. Edited by James H. Cone and Gayraud S. Wilmore. Maryknoll, N.Y.: Orbis, 1993.

Articles

"Kierkegaard on Truth and Subjectivity." *Journal of Religious Thought* 28, no. 1 (1961): 41–56.
"A Theological Conception of the State." *Journal of Church and State* 4, no. 1 (1962): 66–75.
"Majoring in Minors." *Link* 20, no. 9 (1962): 5–8.
"Christian Conscience and Legal Discrimination." *Journal of Religious Thought* 19, no. 2 (1962–63): 157–61.
"Madhva Logic According to the Pramanacandrika." *Journal of Religious Thought* 20, no. 1 (1963–64): 105–14.
"Bergson as a Metaphysical, Epistemological and Religious Thinker." *Journal of Religious Thought* 20, no. 2 (1963–64): 105–14.
"Religious and Political Realism in Kautilya's Arthasastra." *Journal of Religious Thought* 22, no. 2 (1965–66): 153–66.
"Karma-Yoga in Tilak's Gita Rahhaysa." *Journal of Religious Thought* 24, no. 1 (1967–68): 83–98.
"The Black Caucus and the Failure of Christian Theology." *Journal of Religious Thought* 26, no. 2 (1969):15–25.
"Folklore and Religions: The Black Experience." *Journal of Religious Thought* 27, no. 2 (1970): 5–15.
"Black Theology and the Theological Revolution." *Journal of Religious Thought* 28, no. 1 (1971): 5–20.
"Afro-Arab Islam and the Black Revolution." *Journal of Religious Thought* 28, no. 2 (1972): 95–111.
"Black Theology in the Making." *Review and Expositor* 70 (summer 1973): 321–30.
"Religio-Ethical Reflections Upon the Experiential Components of a Philosophy of Black Liberation." *Journal of the Interdenominational Theological Center* 1 (fall 1973): 80–94.
"Black Theological Education: Programming for Liberation." *Christian Century* (6 February 1974): 117–18.
"Theology of Religions: The Black Religious Heritage." *Journal of the Interdenominational Theological Center* 1 (spring 1974): 54–68.

"Le Dieu de l'homme noir." *Lumière and Vie* 23 (November–December 1974): 41–49.

"A Black Ecclesiology of Involvement." *Journal of Religious Thought* 32 (spring–summer 1975): 36–46.

"Black Theological Ethics: A Bibliographical Essay." *Journal of Religious Thought* 3 (spring 1975): 69–109.

"Contextual Theology: Liberation and Indigenization." *Christian Century* 93 (28 January 1976): 64–68.

"Black Liberation Theism." *Journal of Religious Thought* 33 (spring–summer 1976): 25–35.

"Ben Chavis Case." *Journal of Religious Thought* 33 (fall–winter 1976): 5–10.

"Black Theologies and African Theologies." *Insight: A Journal of World Religions* 3 (1978–1979): 14–27.

"Moral Suasion as Nonviolent Direct Action: The Legacy of William Stuart Nelson." *Journal of Religious Thought* 35 (fall–winter 1978–79).

"New Power for the Black Church." *Journal of the Society for Common Insights* 2 (17 November 1978): 63–67.

"The Books That Shape Lives." *Christian Century* (31 January 1979): 108.

"Contextualization of Theology in the New South." With Frederick Herzog. *Journal of Religious Thought* 36 (spring–summer 1979): 54–60.

"The Impact of the Black Church: Sole Surviving Black Institution." *Journal of the Interdenominational Theological Center* 6 (spring 1979): 138–47.

"Christian Liberation Ethics: The Black Experience." *Religion in Life* 48 (summer 1979): 227–35.

"Traditional African Religions and Christian Theology." *Studia Africana* 1 (fall 1979): 206–18.

"A Black Theologian in Mexico." *Journal of Religious Thought* 37 (spring–summer 1980): 15–22.

"Ecumenical Concerns Among National Baptists." *Journal of Ecumenical Studies* 17 (spring 1980): 38–48.

"Liberation Theologies: A Critical Essay." *Journal of the Interdenominational Theological Center* 9 (fall 1981): 85–89.

"Where Do We Go from Here?" *Journal of the Interdenominational Theological Center* 8 (spring 1981): 137–43.

"Gospel Particularity and Global Solidarity." *Grapevine* 14 (June 1982).

"Eine Kreative Antword auf den Rassismus: Die Schwarze Theologie." *Concilium* 171 (1982): 32–40.

"Christian Liberation Ethics: The Black Experience." *Military Chaplain's Review* 2 (summer 1982): 53–60.

"Liberating Theological Education: Can Our Seminaries Be Saved?" *Christian Century* (2–9 February 1983): 98, 113–16.

"Black Religion." *Mid-Stream* 22 (July–October 1983): 378–85.

"The Holy Spirit and Liberation: A Black Perspective." *AME Zion Quarterly Review* 96 (January 1985): 19–28.

"An Afro-American/African Theological Dialogue." *Toronto Journal of Theology* 2 (fall 1986): 172–87.

"Christian-Marxist Conference in Granada, Spain." *Journal of Ecumenical Studies* 25 (fall 1988): 687–89.

"The Quest for Mutuality: Confronting Sexism in the Black Church — Theological Reflections on Mutuality between Black Females and Males." *AME Zion Quarterly Review* 99 (October 1988): 20–29.

"A Christian Response to Evil and Suffering." *Religious Education* 84 (winter 1989): 68–76.

"Let My People Go: The Black/Jewish Ecumenical Dialogue." *Ecumenical Trends* 19 (January 1990): 1–4.

"The Status of Black Catholics." *Journal of Religious Thought* 48 (summer–fall 1991): 73–78.

"Slavery in the Americas: Economic, Cultural, and Religious Consequences." *Journal of the Interdenominational Theological Center* 19 (fall–spring 1991–92): 113–21.

"And We Are Not Saved: A Black Theologian Looks at Theological Education." *Religious Education* 87 (summer 1992): 353–69.

"African Americanism, Afrocentrism and Multiculturalism." *Memphis Theological Seminary Journal* 34 (spring 1996): 3–9.

About J. Deotis Roberts

Prior to his teaching career, J. Deotis Roberts pastored churches in North Carolina, Connecticut, and Glasglow, Scotland. He also ministered to Jamaican and Puerto Rican migrant farm workers in Connecticut and African American migrant workers in Delaware and North Carolina.

After earning his Ph.D. at the University of Edinburgh, he became a professor of theology at Howard University's School of Religion from 1958 to 1980. While on leave from Howard in 1973 to 1974, he was dean of the School of Theology at Virginia Union School of Theology.

In 1980, Dr. Roberts became president of the Interdenominational Theological Center in Atlanta. The ITC is a cluster of theology units representing six denominations. He was also distinguished professor of philosophical theology there.

In 1983 and 1984, he served as adjunct professor of theology at Chandler School of Theology at Emory University and Columbia Seminary, Atlanta, Georgia. Also in 1984, he was appointed distinguished professor of philosophical theology at Eastern Baptist Theological Seminary in Philadelphia and served there until 1998.

In 1998, he was appointed research professor of Christian theology at Duke Divinity School, where he served until 2001. In 2001 and 2002, he was distinguished visiting scholar at Baylor University in the Department of Religion.

In addition to his teaching career, J. Deotis Roberts was also the co-founder of the Black Theology Movement, editor of the *Journal of Religious Thought* (1974–1980), founder and president of the Foundation for Religious and Educational Exchange (1984–1994), and president of the American Theological Society (1994–1995). He has authored fourteen books and more than a hundred articles and essays. In 1994, the University of Edinburgh awarded Roberts the D.Litt. (Doctor of Letters) degree for outstanding contributions to the fields of systematic, philosophical, and black theology.

Index

African ritual, symbolism of,
132–33
Africans
acceptance of Western
philosophies and religion,
148
Bible, understanding of,
120
Christianity, acceptance of,
118–19
decultration of, 118
physiological differences
among, 108–9
religion, propensity
toward, 119
religious thinking of, 130–
36
time concepts, 133–34
uprooting of, 118
African society, sociopolitical
organization of, 137–38
African Theological Journal,
158
African theology, 150–52
biblical interpretation,
156–57
epistemology, 154–56
quest for, 152–54
tradition, 157–59
See also black/African
theologies
African Traditional Religion
(Parrinder), 104
Afro-American Christianity
versus religion of black
power, 33–34
afterlife, 69–70

The Akan Doctrine of God
(Danquah), 105
Alves, Rubem, *A Theology of
Human Hope*, 49
Amos, 13
5:21, 79
5:23–24, 79
Anabaptists, 50
ancestors, 162
veneration of, 100, 142
antebellum period, 122
Aristotle, 19, 131
Asian religions, 98, 105–6
Association of Theological
Schools (ATS), 181, 184–
85
atheism, 169
Augustine, 14
auto-ethnography, 112
of African religions, 106

Baillie, John, 201
Ballie, D. M., *God Was in
Christ*, 163
Baluba, 102
Bambara people, Komo
society, 111
Bantu people, 102, 131–32
Bantu Philosophy (Tempels),
102
baptism, 65
Barth, Karl, 42, 149, 154
state, view of, 16–18,
22
Bell, Derrick, 182

Peter, view of government, 14
phenomenological studies of
    religion, 149–50
Philemon
    1:16, 79
Platonic/Aristotelian tradi-
    tion, 69, 131–32, 155,
    156
Plessy decision, 27
Plowshares toward
    globalization, 196–97
political economy, black
    church and, 84–85
political order, 13–14
politics, theology and, 6
Politics of God (Washington),
    126
polytheistic religions versus
    monotheistic religions,
    99. *See also* African
    religions
Pontifical Commission
    Iustitia et Pax, 93
population, limiting, 39
power, 14
    and justice, subordination
        to, 20–21
    Machiavellian view of, 20
    moral content of, 21
    myth and, 135
    pride of, 47
    sovereign power, 21
pragmatism, 8–9
Prayer (Heiller), 149
preachers, 63–65
prejudice, 24–25
pride, 14, 18, 47

Primal Vision (Taylor), 102,
    104
Primitive Culture (Taylor),
    99
primitive religions versus
    redemptive religions, 100
Principles of Sociology
    (Spencer), 100
prophecy, truthfulness of, 34
protest, faith and, 82
Protestant ethics, 173
Protestants, 146, 149–50

*The Quest for a Black
    Theology* (Roberts and
    Gardiner), 153

race discrimination versus
    race distinction, 27–28
race relations
    breakthrough in, 193
    Christian way, 28
    status of, 179, 185
    See also racism
racial prejudice, origins of,
    24
racial superiority, 24, 25
racism, 43–44
    benign neglect, 59–60
    black/African theologies,
        influence on, 159
    black psyche, effects on,
        187
    as cultural, institutional,
        and systematic evil, 56
    incidence of, 180–81